HOW TO REPLACE & INSTALL FLOORS & FLOOR COVERINGS

Created and designed by the
editorial staff of ORTHO Books

Project Editor
Diane Snow

Writers
B. Gay Ballard
Robert J. Beckstrom
Harriett L. Kirk

Designers
Craig Bergquist
Christine Dunham

Illustrator
Edith Allgood

Photographers
Laurie A. Black
Stephen Marley

Photographic Stylist
Sara Slavin

Ortho Books

Publisher
Robert L. Iacopi

Editorial Director
Min S. Yee

Managing Editors
Anne Coolman
Michael D. Smith

System Manager
Mark Zielinski

Senior Editor
Sally W. Smith

Editors
Jim Beley
Diane Snow
Deni Stein

System Assistant
William F. Yusavage

Production Manager
Laurie Sheldon

Photographers
Laurie A. Black
Michael D. McKinley

Photo Editors
Anne Dickson-Pederson
Pam Peirce

Production Editor
Alice E. Mace

Production Assistant
Darcie S. Furlan

National Sales Manager
Garry P. Wellman

Operations/Distribution
William T. Pletcher

Operations Assistant
Donna M. White

Administrative Assistant
Georgiann Wright

Address all inquiries to
Ortho Books
Chevron Chemical Company
Consumer Products Division
575 Market Street
San Francisco, CA 94105

Chevron Chemical Company
575 Market Street, San Francisco, CA 94105

Acknowledgments

Photography

Front Cover, page 14 (bottom):
Michael LaMotte
Pages 1, 4, 6, 7, 9, 11, 22, 29, 38, 58: Laurie A. Black
Pages 8, 10, 16, 17, 23, 28:
Stephen Marley
Pages 14 (top, middle), 15 (top, middle): American Parquet Assoc., Magnolia, AK
Page 15 (bottom): Oak Flooring Institute, Memphis, TN
Pages 20, 21 (middle, bottom left), 26, 27, 32, 33: Alan Copeland
Page 21 (top): Natural Vinyl Floor Co., Inc., Florence, AL
Page 21 (bottom right): Jason/Perelli, Fairfield, NJ

Designers, Architects, Builders

Pages 1, 7: Phillip Emminger, Lafayette, CA
Pages 4, 28: Dan Phipps & Assoc., San Francisco, CA
Pages 6, 29: Joeve Wilkinson, Walnut Creek, CA
Page 8: Trey Hoagland & Marc Hamman, San Francisco, CA
Page 9: Barbara Piepergerdes, Walnut Creek, CA
Page 10: Craig Leavitt & Stephen Weaver, San Francisco, CA
Page 11: Robert H. Hersey, A.I.A., San Francisco, CA
Page 16: David Smith, Sausalito, CA
Page 17: Ron Pimentel, San Francisco, CA
Page 22: The Finishing Touch, Pacifica, CA
Page 23: Molly McGowan, Oakland, CA
Pages 38, 58: Robert Steffy, San Francisco, CA

Photographic Styling Assistance

Kathryn Hadley
San Francisco, CA

Props

Abbey Carpets
Amsterdam Corporation
C. W. Welch
Conklin Bros.
Floor Service Supply Co.
Floorcraft
Floordesigns, Inc.
Hans Kenkert
Terra Bella
Tilecraft Ltd.

Consultants

Rich Antonchuk
A. Antonchuk
San Francisco, CA

Pat Brook
Pleasant Hill, CA

Claire Carter
Angelica Designers
Orinda, CA

Lloyd Malfatti
Garland-White & Co.
Union City, CA

Bill McCready
Monroe Schneider
South San Francisco, CA

Joe McDaniel
The Ceramic Tile Store
Concord, CA

David Nikhazy
Contra Costa Tile
Walnut Creek, CA

Michael Pisani
Euro-Cal Trading, Inc.
Concord, CA

Ray Schneider
Golden State Flooring
Brisbane, CA

Malcom Rea
Pacific Flooring Supply
Emeryville, CA

Andy Solari
Northern California Floor Covering Industry Fund
San Francisco, CA

Emil Te Groen
Northern California Ceramic Tile Industry
San Francisco, CA

Illustration Assistance

Charles Fuhrman
Ron Hildebrand
Phillip Hocking
Marty Walton

Copyediting and Proofreading

Editcetera
Berkeley, CA

Typesetting

Vera Allen Composition
Castro Valley, CA

Color Separation

Color Tech
Redwood City, CA

Special Thanks:

Armstrong World Industries, Inc.
Lancaster, PA
 Helen P. Misogianes
 Robert C. de Camara

Azrock Floor
San Antonio, TX
 Joe Condril

Peace Flooring Company
Magnolia, AK

Public Relations for the Tile Council of America
Mahwah, NJ
 Lis King

The San Francisco Decorator Showcase 1983
San Francisco, CA

Lyle Beckstrom
William and Karin Bodman
Mr. and Mrs. Richard M. Carroll
Patricia Davenport
Albert Duke
Mr. and Mrs. Paul Epstein
David and Elizabeth Nelson
James and Barbara Piepergerdes
Al Pollard
Sandra and Dan Webster

Front cover

Your choice of flooring materials is rich with variety, including options for color, texture, pattern, and scale. Sheet goods such as carpet, tile units such as ceramic or parquet, or strip materials such as wood plank, comprise some of the flooring types available to you.

Title Page

Dark wood flooring and crisp white woodwork come together in high contrast to generate a special, bright quality of warmth and cozy calm in this room. Wood flooring is practical, comfortable, and attractive, making it a popular choice for floors in any room of your home.

Back cover

The ambience of rooms and spaces develops out of the interplay between finish treatments, furnishings, and functions—all of which work together to create a harmonious whole. Whether natural materials, such as wood or tile, or man-made ones such as resilients or carpet, the floor plays a key role in how the room looks, feels, and works.

HOW TO REPLACE & INSTALL FLOORS & FLOOR COVERINGS

Chapter 1

Chapter 2

Chapter 3

SELECTION

Whether you're considering wood, resilient,
masonry, or carpet flooring, the first step
toward its successful installation is selection.
Use the photographs, illustrations, and charts
in this chapter to get the process underway.

The installation of new flooring is always a dramatic event. Because a floor is such a large surface area and its installation is often the last step in a redecorating or remodeling project, it can seem as if a new floor suddenly and magically transforms the room. It pulls together all the other elements—paint, wallpaper, fixtures, and trim—into one harmonious whole.

While the installation itself seems to produce an instant transformation, it is actually part of a longer process consisting of three distinct phases: selection, preparation, and installation. The three chapters of this book are organized around these three phases. Their purpose is to help you make wise decisions and use appropriate skills in all three phases, no matter what type of new flooring you select, how much of the work you do yourself, or how extensively you choose to engage professional help.

The first chapter helps you with the selection phase in two ways. First, it gives you a broad perspective by treating the floor as a major design element in each room and by discussing the factors you'll want to consider in making your selection. Second, it offers you specific options from which to choose. Your selection adventure begins on the next four pages with an overview of floors in general. This is followed by four sections that

◄

In this attic workspace, granite tile flooring restates the crisp, gable-beamed ceiling. When a floor's design enhances existing architectural elements, it helps create harmony and vibrancy within the space. And when carefully chosen for color, texture, and pattern, flooring materials—even those that may seem cool and hard—can provide richness and ambient warmth.

cover each category of flooring materials—wood, resilient, ceramic, and carpet—in greater depth, helping you to narrow your choices and move toward a final selection of material that is right for your floor. The chapter ends by offering guidelines for working effectively with professionals, measuring your room, and estimating the amount and cost of materials.

Chapter 2 focuses on the critical process of preparing a floor surface for new finish flooring. It reviews the anatomy of both wood-frame and concrete floors, and outlines specific preparation requirements for laying each type of flooring material over various existing floor conditions. Then it illustrates how to remove flooring and trim, make surface repairs to existing floors, and add whatever underlayment may be needed. The chapter also presents the techniques for handling and storing each type of material, and the tools that will be needed for installing it.

Chapter 3 covers the installation steps for each type of flooring material, from planning the layout and marking the lines that guide the installation to attaching the final piece of trim. Whether you are a committed do-it-yourselfer or prefer to hand the details of installation to someone else, you can use this chapter (as well as Chapter 2) in two ways: as a guide for providing professionals with important information about your floor and your preferences or as a step-by-step workbook to guide you through those phases yourself.

Once again, you'll find that a successful floor installation requires careful attention to all three phases: selection, preparation, and installation. You may discover that you enjoy the process almost as much as that final day when you stand in the middle of your new floor, admire the work, and enjoy the finished effect.

A PERSPECTIVE ON FLOORS

Floors are a strong design element in your house, often setting the tone or feeling for the whole environment. Because they form the ground plane and are a major horizontal element of the room, floors have the potential to integrate space and become the foundation for your interior design. Whether subtle or dramatic, a floor can direct how a room is used, establish its ambience, and tie its design elements together.

Because floors are such an important part of a room's design, you'll want to select new flooring carefully. Your concept of beauty is constantly evolving and changing, and the simpler the floor treatment, the more flexibility you'll have in the room's design and use over time. It is much easier and less expensive to change the color of your walls, or to introduce new furnishings and accessories, than it is to install a new floor. So select your flooring material with an eye on the future, as well as on your current inclinations. If you opt for a dramatic and exciting design and decide that you want to use the floor to create it, then be bold. Use the floor as the keynote for the design, and let the other elements and features—furniture, lighting, and accessories—play a supporting role.

As a general guide, good design is simple design—although simplicity isn't always easy to achieve. It requires a high level of restraint, thoughtfulness in planning, and care in execution.

Light and dark. A light floor, like light ceilings and walls, will make a room look more spacious and open by reflecting more of the available natural light, and more artificial light as well. Darker tones tend to contract and confine space, but can also make the room appear warmer and more intimate or cozy.

Color. Almost as much as light or dark, color has the power to affect the ambience or atmosphere of a room. More than any other element, it can unify an interior design throughout the house. The same color or the same color theme, used in successive rooms, helps to integrate interior spaces—even in a house that combines different design styles.

Different colors create different effects, and color preferences are very personal. Some color preferences, however, are actually color "prejudices." They can be as simple as "I need dark colors in my house because I have small children," or "I always wanted a pink room when I was young." If pink is a favorite color from your past, you'll want to make sure it will be an enduring favorite before you do the whole house in it. By the same token, dark colors don't always hide dirt, and they aren't always easier to keep clean. If you're unsure of the design or color direction you'd like to take, you may want to consult with a professional interior designer. Good designers can help you define just what it is you want, and show you how to accomplish it.

Below: Two-by-two-foot-square solid vinyl tiles give this living room an elegant simplicity that can be dressed up or down. Softly marbled celadon and white form a neutral ground for furnishings. *Right:* Wood used top and bottom sandwiches bright white walls and bed coverings, which sparkle against the dark wood strip floor.

Pattern and scale. Again, simplicity is the key to good design when working with pattern and scale. Large patterns tend to decrease the apparent size of a room, especially if the pattern contains several colors. Busy patterns can distract from other design elements, and may make it harder to change the room in the future. An effective floor pattern need not vie for attention—it can simply provide a background for other, more flexible expressions of taste.

Scale refers to the proportional relationships of design elements. It is especially important when single units, such as tiles or stones, are used. For example, there is a particularly pleasing relationship between the size of tile or stone units, the width of grout lines, and the size of the room. Professional installers have charts which outline these relationships, so that the floor pattern looks proportional to the room, and therefore, visually balanced and pleasant.

Texture. Texture can also affect the room's ambience. For instance, a stone floor in a small, dark room may feel cool and inviting in the desert states, but more like a chilly dungeon in northeastern areas. When flooring materials have to change from room to room for practical reasons, you can still retain a unified design by keeping the color consistent and just changing the texture—for example, by using ceramic tile in the kitchen next to a carpet of the same or similar color in adjoining rooms. Some carpet manufacturers offer the same color carpet in a variety of textures or weights: heavy-duty, low-loop pile for the dining room or playroom; luxurious plush for the living room; and less expensive, less durable pile for a bedroom where the traffic tends to be light. You can also use texture to practical advantage. For rooms where the floor may get wet—kitchens, bathrooms, laundry rooms, and entryways—choose a material with enough texture to prevent slipping.

People. At the heart of the matter, rooms are for living. They create the background for people and the range of activities they engage in. The purpose of the design, planning, and selection phase is to create the most enjoyable room possible for the people who will use it. The pages that follow will help you accomplish this goal.

For each of the four main types of flooring materials—wood, resilient, ceramic and other masonry, and carpet—you'll find a six-page section describing and illustrating the nature of the material, its aesthetic and functional qualities, and special characteristics of the different forms in which the material is sold.

Use these sections in two ways: (1) to compare and select among the four major categories of flooring materials, and (2) to make more specific selections within a category. The chapter is designed for both browsing and more careful reading. Use it both ways, and enjoy creating a new environment with your new floor.

Below: A tan-on-black color theme gives substance to this bedroom without sacrificing its airy quality. The simply-patterned carpet ties together walls and furniture, while accessories provide bright highlights. *Right:* Large-scale white ceramic tiles in a white grout grid, provides visual continuity and expands the apparent size of this kitchen.

CONSIDERING
WOOD FLOORS

The warmth, beauty, and durability of wood make it one of the most popular of flooring materials. Wood can add a special feeling of quality, permanence, and livability to any room, and will last the lifetime of the house, if properly installed. If it is well protected and cared for, it will never have to be refinished, but will only look better as it takes on the patina of age. Wood is also an insulating material; and it is comfortable to walk on, due to its natural resilience.

Although wood materials can be attractive in any area in the house, you'll want to look carefully at the room's environmental conditions when you're considering wood materials. Will the room be subject to a great deal of moisture? Kitchens and bathrooms usually have high humidity conditions, which can cause wood flooring to swell, and possibly even buckle if the finish is moisture-permeable. If the room has a good ventilation system, room humidity probably won't affect the flooring. But if a lot of moisture tends to collect, a different material might be a better option. Water from spills or traffic can cause wood materials to stain, warp, or even rot if the surface finish can't resist it, and if enough of it collects. A waterproof finish like polyurethane can protect wood materials from these conditions.

Wood materials are also subject to scratches and surface abrasion. If the area you're considering collects a lot of sand or grit from traffic (in a beach house, for example), you should consider using a very dense hardwood finished with several coats of a durable wear-resistant surface finish.

When you counterbalance your understanding of the nature of wood material with the functions of the room where you're considering installing it, you're more apt to make the most appropriate selection.

Below: Wide planking, plugged and toned dark, ties together the furnishings, bookcases, and architectural trim detailing of this traditional room, creating a unified and harmonious design theme. *Right:* Natural wood floors, along with soft and simple furniture lines, amplify the pleasant qualities of this room's natural light.

WOOD FLOORS

Planning and design issues for wood flooring vary with the materials you're considering—linear materials like strip and plank, or square units like wood block or parquet. Linear materials make a strong directional statement by creating lines that run either the length or width of the room. Because this direction is so forcefully implicit in the material, you can use it either to enhance or alter the room's visual proportions. For example, a proportionally narrow, long room will look wider and more spacious if you run the strips or planks across the width.

(Check the direction of the joists; strip materials should run perpendicular to them.) On the other hand, wood block or parquet tiles make no directional statement, but do provide a very definite pattern, or even a complex mosaic.

With both types of wood materials, you have a full range of detail options. You may want to punctuate the flooring field by contrasting it with a special border. If that border is very wide, the flooring field becomes an area in its own right, with the border serving as a tran-

Kitchens are typically special areas where work joins pleasure—an easy gathering place for family and friends. Wood lends its inherent feeling of warmth and welcome, effectively counterbalancing the cool feeling of appliances and slick counter surfaces and softening the hard-edged effect of cabinetry.

Living rooms are often reserved for entertaining and may be maintained as the most formal room of the house. Yet they might be expected to perform other functions as well: workspace, play area, family room, or a place for quiet relaxation. Wood flooring works well in any of these situations with equal beauty and charm.

sition to it. You can also "wrap" the floor up the wall with a classic, high baseboard, finished in the same tone as the flooring. Or you can create a crisp horizontal ground plane that joins the wall but remains quite distinct from it—baseboards, harmonizing with the wall color, will give you that effect. The profile of a baseboard as well as its height and color have a distinct effect on the overall feeling of a room.

The finished floor's tone and sheen also contribute to the room's ambient quality. Dark, lustrous floors feel heavy and grounded; they tend to contract the apparent size of the space. Lighter matte finishes create an expansive feeling of space.

When making your selections, think of the overall visual and ambient effect you'd like the room to have. Whatever choice you make—narrow strips, wide planks, or an intricate pattern of parquet; light or dark wood, textured or smooth, lustrous or matte—wood is one of the most beautiful and practical solutions for any floor in your house.

Bedrooms are generally meant to be restful—at least for a certain portion of the day—giving a feeling of calm, coziness, and quietude. At other times, they might be used for hobbies, dressing, personal grooming, and concentrated study or work. Wood floors provide a practical and attractive background for these activities and render a pleasant feeling of ease and comfort in bedroom spaces.

Because bathrooms tend to be small spaces with particular practical requirements, floor surfaces need to be easy to clean and able to resist water. If appropriately finished and thoroughly sealed, wood flooring can successfully meet this requirement while maintaining its natural beauty.

WOOD MATERIALS

Parquet tile. Short lengths of wood define four bands in each tile, giving an overall linear effect.

Parquet tile. A four-square pattern in each tile gives the finish floor a basket weave effect.

Tongue-and-groove strip flooring, finished in light tones, creates the classic look of wood floors.

Although not all woods are specially milled for flooring purposes, many species of wood can be used for floors. This chart deals with those species commonly milled specifically for flooring. Your choice may depend on what is traditionally used in your part of the country—regionally produced species are usually more readily available, and are sometimes less expensive than species that have to be shipped long distances.

Various grading systems are used for different species. In general, the higher grades are considered to have the best quality in terms of strength, appearance, regularity, and so on. But you may prefer the knots, streaks, and spots of one of the lesser grades. Flooring is milled in several thicknesses, and comes in two forms: tongue-and-groove, (which gives a strong interlocking joint in which the nails are concealed), or square-edge (which must be nailed through the floor's visible surface).

Some flooring materials can be purchased prefinished: the sealers and

WOOD FLOORING MATERIALS

	Color	Grain
HARDWOODS		
Red Oak	Tan to light pink.	Highly figured.
White Oak	Light tan to yellow.	Straight to highly figured.
Teak	Light to dark browns and reds.	Generally straight, and uniform; some species have wild grain.
Walnut	Reddish or chocolate brown to light tan.	Low to highly figured, burly.
Maple	Light honey to near white.	Fine and close.
Pecan/Hickory	Honey brown to light pink.	Character marked, open.
SOFTWOODS		
Pine	White to golden.	Vertical or flat, open.
Douglas Fir	Golden orange.	Flat grain wavy and open; vertical grain very straight.
Redwood	Pink to rosy.	Flat grain open and wavy; vertical grain very uniform.

waxes are baked on at the mill. The range of species and stains sold is limited, however, and these materials are more expensive than most unfinished flooring. But you do save the time it takes to apply finishes.

Most people think of hardwood when they think of wood floors, although some softwoods are similarly dense and durable. Hardwood and softwood are terms describing botanical characteristics of the wood rather than its texture or density. The softer woods tend to dent, but you may prize their patina—the look of age and use.

Each species has a specific color range, grain pattern, texture, and density—all these characteristics contribute to the look and feel of the finished floor. And, of course, some woods can be stained in a wide range of tones. The chart on these two pages lists the characteristics of various wood species. Use it to compare and contrast the many different wood species, and to get an overview of some of your many options.

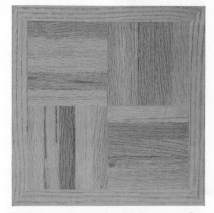

Parquet tile. A four-square pattern set inside a perimeter band, gives the effect of a weave-within-a-grid.

Texture and Density	Comments
Medium density.	Most popular flooring wood, widely available, stains and finishes well.
Medium density.	Similar to red oak in working and finishing characteristics.
Smooth texture, high density.	Contains natural moisture-resistant oils; oil-based finishes work best.
Uniformly hard and dense.	Takes finish coats uniformly, makes attractive borders and accent strips.
Uniformly fine texture.	Extremely hard underfoot, durable, similar to beech.
Uniformly hard and dense.	Hardest wood flooring; species are interchangeable.
Soft to medium density; gains patina of dents.	Some pines are unacceptably soft for flooring applications.
Flat grain variable and uneven density; vertical grain smooth and even texture.	Flat grain takes stain unevenly; vertical grain stains uniformly.
Soft to medium density; gains patina of dents.	Rich deep color when sealed, prone to splintering.

Parquet tile. A basic four-square pattern within each tile gives a simple, wood block effect.

Tongue-and-groove random-width plank flooring, plugged with contrasting wood, gives a warm, traditional effect.

RESILIENT FLOORS

Resilient materials—whether glossy, or matte-surfaced, lightly mottled or highly textured, monochromatic or marbleized—can be used to create an expansive, elegant quality in any room. They are highly versatile for all areas of the house, and provide an easy visual continuity between individual spaces or rooms, while offering good functional characteristics.

Resilient materials are available in a wide range of colors and patterns, offering options that span from subtle and refined to bold and dramatic. In quiet colors and patterns, resilient materials have the potential for understatement at its best, and used in combination with area rugs, they are suitable for any type of room and for any kind of setting.

Functionally, these materials create a floor that is easy to maintain, durable, and comfortable underfoot. They are practical, relatively inexpensive, easy to install (especially tile materials), and can be laid over many existing floor surfaces, including directly over concrete.

When considering using resilient flooring in a particular room, you will want to keep in mind some of the material's natural qualities—both its advantages and limitations. A major attribute of resilient flooring materials is that they are made to resist moisture. However, joints (between tiles) and seams (between abutting sheets) are potential access points for water, spills, and grime to seep under the floor. Careful installation helps to avoid this potential problem, allowing you to take full advantage of the flooring's water-resistant quality.

Because these materials are produced in light gauges, any subsurface defects or irregularities will show up in the finish floor. Unless the subsurface is properly prepared, sooner or later traffic moving through the room will abrade the finish surface over these irregularities and wear out the flooring in these areas. If you can't properly smooth and prepare the subsurface, you may want to consider choosing a different type of material.

When planning a resilient floor for a particular room, you'll want to take advantage of the material's shape—its manufactured form—and use it as part of your design. The illustrations and discussion on the next pages will help you do this.

Below: Dramatic effects can be achieved with simple materials when you let your imagination wing free. Black and white resilient tiles look lively in a carefully designed random pattern. *Right:* Against high-gloss white woodwork and fresh exterior views, Pirelli flooring provides crisp contrast, while raised studs give both pattern and traction.

RESILIENT FLOORS

The illustrations below give you an idea of how the same type of material can be effectively used in rooms with very different functions—in each instance, creating a particular ambient effect. When using resilient materials in any room, there are a number of planning and design issues to keep in mind.

These issues differ depending on whether you're considering sheet goods or tile units. Sheet goods are available in a limited number of widths. If your room is larger than the sheet's width, you'll have to seam two pieces together, and these seam placements will affect both the look and performance of your finish floor. Because the continuity of sheet flooring is a special feature worth retaining, you can minimize the visibility of seams by placing them in secondary areas of the room. The seam will be essentially invisible if you plan to run it along an existing line in the surface pattern.

Tile units present different design possibilities. Tiles can be laid out in a square-grid format oriented square to the room, or laid out on a diagonal grid. The pattern can include special borders, create a checker-board effect, or even show a random design. The section on

Kitchens are generally heavily-trafficked, high-activity areas where soil and spills are a common occurrence. Where practicality and easy maintenance are important considerations, resilient materials are an excellent choice. Because there is such a wide range of colors, patterns, and surface textures to choose from, almost any design theme can be carried out.

Resilient materials are reputed for their no-nonsense practicality. However, because they are man-made materials, they can also be fabricated to emulate more expensive natural materials in a very satisfactory way. Where a beautiful visual effect is the primary design goal, and practicality runs a close second, carefully chosen resilient materials can lend a striking elegance and refinement to any room.

layout (pages 60–61) will help you make planning decisions for resilient tiles.

For both sheet and tile floors, pattern (and its scale), surface texture, and color will play a combined role in the final look of the room. Pattern and scale work together to make a space feel expansive, calm, lively, busy, or cramped. Large floor areas can accommodate a larger-scaled pattern without overwhelming the room. But small rooms, like bathrooms, need a simple pattern of smaller scale if the floor is to create a pleasant visual effect.

Texture is often an inherent part of the pattern. An embossed texture in the pattern itself highlights and punctuates the pattern more than a smooth surface. The shapes that make up the pattern also affect the overall feeling of design. Curved shapes activate each other in a swirl of motion; angular shapes oppose and hold each other in place; geometric shapes reside with each other to form an integrated field. Whenever you are selecting patterns, bear these principles in mind so that you will choose those that are in harmony with your overall design goals.

Inexpensive and easy-to-install materials, such as 12-inch-square white resilient tiles, can give any room a warm and pleasant graciousness. Particularly when bedrooms serve several functions, resilient materials may be a worthwhile choice—as much from an aesthetic standpoint as from a practical one.

Bathroom cabinetry and fixtures are often clean-lined, slick-surfaced, cool-feeling elements, which could suggest a high-tech approach to the design scheme. Resilient flooring materials can effectively create it. Many resilient materials are highly resistant to water, making them an especially appropriate choice for bathroom spaces.

RESILIENT MATERIALS

Inexpensive resilient tile materials can attractively simulate grouted ceramic or masonry flooring.

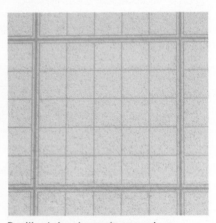

Resilient sheet goods come in a wide variety of patterns such as this grid-over-grid design.

Resilient flooring materials include man-made compounds, plus a few natural products. Your choice will certainly be guided by cost, but other factors will also shape your final selection; these are listed in the chart below. Products manufactured from a natural material base—such as cork, rubber, and wood—are generally more expensive than the entirely man-made products, with the exception of top-of-the-line solid vinyl. Where you plan to install the floor is an important consideration in selection. Some materials are more resistant than others to grease and oil, water, temper-

RESILIENT FLOORING MATERIALS

	Solid Vinyl and Cushioned Vinyl	Vinyl Composition
Color, Pattern, and Texture	Wide range of colors and patterns; may be laminated with fabric, wood, marble chips; smooth or embossed surfaces.	Many colors and patterns, colors marbleized or solid, smooth or embossed surfaces.
Durability	Grease and oil resistant; susceptible to heat; cushioned vinyl may dent. Medium to heavy-duty gauges.	Good for damp areas, properly seamed. Good resistance to chemicals. Light-, medium-, and heavy-duty gauges.
Resiliency	Cushioned materials are very comfortable underfoot. Good sound insulation.	Not as resilient or sound insulating as solid vinyl.
Maintenance Requirements	Use solvent-based or water-based waxes and polishes. Damp mop; avoid excess water.	Use water-based products only.
Relative Cost	High.	Low to medium.

In neutral, monochromatic tones, pattern can be more intricate without appearing overwhelmingly busy.

Resilient sheet goods, as well as tiles, can attractively simulate natural materials, such as this ceramic tile design.

ature changes, denting, or chemicals. For instance, rubber is an excellent choice for a darkroom because it is especially chemical-resistant. On the other hand, it doesn't resist grease and oil well, so it may not be the best choice for kitchens. Unless they have cushion backing, the lighter-gauge flexible resilients will mold to any irregularities in the subfloor; the smoothness of the subsurface underlayment for the floor is crucial. The chart lists the characteristics of different resilient materials to help you make the best selection for your particular flooring needs.

Resilient tiles made of solid vinyl effectively simulate pearl, creating a subtle, luminescent, marbleized effect.

Rubber	Vinyl-Coated Cork	Polyurethane Wood
Handful of solid and marbleized colors; surface may be smooth, ribbed, or studded.	Limited range of natural cork colors; smooth surfaces.	Limited range of wood grain and colors; smooth surfaces.
Good for damp areas. Very good resistance to most chemicals. Susceptible to grease and oil stains. Heavy-duty gauges.	Grease and oil resistant, susceptible to heat; cushioned vinyl may dent. Medium- to heavy-duty gauges.	Excellent resistance to dents. Heavy-duty gauges.
Very comfortable underfoot. Good sound insulation.	Very comfortable underfoot. Good sound insulation.	Hard underfoot. Good sound insulation.
Use water-based products only. Requires frequent polishing.	Use solvent-based or water-based waxes and polishes. Damp mop; avoid excess water.	Use water-based products; avoid excess water.
Medium to high.	Highest.	Medium to high.

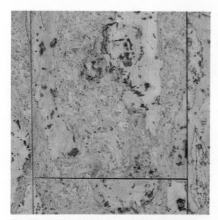

Resilient tile can be made of natural materials such as cork or leather, giving the floor a rich texture.

Patterned resilient sheet goods give the effect of solid color when the pattern is created by tiny, random elements.

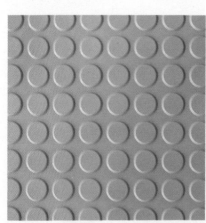

Resilient sheet goods include rubber materials, which are available in a variety of colors and configurations.

CERAMIC & MASONRY FLOORS

Ceramic tiles and other masonry flooring, such as brick and stone, are natural and durable materials that create a feeling of tradition, permanence, and substance in a room. Depending on the type of material you select—rustic "country" brick, rich elegant marble, or casual but tailored quarry—masonry tiles set the level of a room's formality and its style. They can be used in any room in the house, and require relatively little attention once they are installed. Each adds special qualities to the character of the room, but because they are all made of earth materials, they also share some common characteristics which should be kept in mind—along with the room's function—when considering masonry.

First, masonry materials tend to be cool to the touch, an advantage in hot weather, but a possible source of discomfort in cold climates (unless they are installed over a radiant heating system or are used to collect solar heat). Because they are also heavier than most types of flooring, wood-frame subfloors may have to be reinforced to carry the extra weight. The thicker materials will also raise the floor level; this may make them impractical where floor levels are established and raised transitions to other rooms might be awkward.

Ceramic tiles with glazed surfaces are water-resistant. The grout lines between them, however, are not—unless they are carefully sealed. Unglazed surfaces are water-permeable, although you can either wax or seal them against water absorption.

Masonry materials tend to be slippery when wet; choose products with enough surface texture to provide adequate traction. Masonry also tends to deflect sound, rather than absorb it. If the acoustics of the room are important, use unglazed or textured materials, which will absorb sound best. You may also want to consider a different type of material.

By their nature, ceramic and other masonry materials are unit materials, which, when assembled together over the floor's expanse, create a pattern. You'll want to include this—and other design issues described on the next pages—in your selection considerations.

Below: Three different tile sizes join to form a larger pattern, punctuated by slate-colored grout. Hand-hewn tiles provide an equally attractive background for old or new furniture and cabinetry. *Right:* Blue and white ceramic tiles repeat the clean cabinetry lines above. Although the tiles look mosaic, each tile has its own grid glazed within it.

CERAMIC & MASONRY FLOORS

The planning and design issues for ceramic tile, brick, and stone are relatively straightforward. The size of the tile and its shape, color, and surface texture work in tandem with the pattern and color of grout lines to form an ordered geometric grid. The color of the grout, relative to the color of the tile surface—depending on whether they are contrasting or monochromatic—either accentuates the grid pattern or minimizes its visibility. The scale of the tile creates an effect that varies with the scale of the room. For example, in a large room, small units tend to visually blend together so that they appear as an even pattern across the floor. On the other hand, large tiles will stand out as distinct units. In a small room, quarry tiles will seem extraordinarily large and bold, and will tend to jump expressively forward, whereas ceramic mosaic tiles will look relatively quiet, and appropriately in scale.

Because a tile floor is composed of unit pieces, pat-

Traditionally, masonry materials have enjoyed high esteem as a flooring choice. They elicit the feeling of substance, create a pleasing visual rhythm, and lend a sense of scale to the space—all of which can be valuable design features. Although they sometimes require special care, their ambient qualities are appreciably receptive, homey, and attractively comfortable.

An orderly grid of hard-surfaced, glazed ceramic tiles can present a tone of coolly refined formality in a living room. The effect is tailored, though tensioned and controlled. An expansive island of warm, plush carpet defines the main gathering area, beckoning you to cross the tile boundary, stretch out, and relax.

tern is a dominant aspect in the flooring design. Tiles of contrasting color can be used effectively to set a special pattern into the new flooring, defining or separating spaces. This pattern may feature a wide border, a narrow band, or a geometric design or mosaic in the center of the room. Grout lines themselves can be part of the floor's design. The net effect of grout lines in the same color as the tiles is a clean-lined, tailored floor with a subdued grid of intersecting lines. If a contrasting grout color is used, the grid itself is highlighted and stands out.

Surface finish, texture, and color also play a role in the room's design. Dimpled or pocked tile looks hand-worked and casual. Smooth glazed tiles tend to look more austere and refined. Color options range from vivid hues to neutral and natural tones. As with other types of flooring, the more natural and neutral the color, the more flexible the space when co-ordinating masonry materials with other design elements.

The rhythm of the grout-line grid, and the smooth, substantial look of terra cotta quarry tile, creates an attractive effect in a softly and simply furnished bedroom. Natural earth tones visually link indoor living areas with the landscape outside, rendering an inviting, cool-to-the-touch, but warm-to-the-eye living space.

Natural masonry materials, such as slate, can be strikingly beautiful as a flooring material, giving this bathroom a sophisticated simplicity. Though expensive, masonry materials can achieve high returns in design for a small investment in dollars when they are used in small spaces. When properly finished, the surface won't be harmed by water and the material's inherent texture provides traction underfoot.

CERAMIC & MASONRY MATERIALS

Smooth, low-sheen glazed ceramic tiles of medium scale, set with contrasting grout.

Installing a ceramic, brick, or stone floor requires an investment of time, money, and effort. The floor isn't likely to be replaced for a long time. You will want to take special care in selecting the right material for your floor. To help you narrow the range of choices, consider your selection from two points of view: first, the substructure's inherent strength; and second, the new material's characteristics.

With masonry materials, there are some special structural considerations. The additional weight of the heavier of these materials can overstress a wood-frame floor and even the foundation below it unless they are designed to carry the load. For concrete slabs, weight isn't an issue.

CERAMIC, BRICK, & STONE FLOORING MATERIALS

	Ceramic Tile and Ceramic Mosaics	Quarry Tile and Pavers
Sizes and Shapes	1" to 6" ceramic mosaic, usually ¼" thick. 4" to 10" ceramic tile, from ⅜" to ½" thick. Squares, rectangles, other geometric shapes. Rounded or squared edges.	4" to 12" units, ⅜" to ⅞" thick. Squares, rectangles, and random, roughly geometrical shapes.
Colors and Textures	Wide variety of brilliant and muted colors. Glossy, matte, and textured non-slip. Ceramic mosaics may be porcelain, china, or glass.	Natural earth tones, some blues and greens. Mexican pavers can be stained almost any color. Matte or textured non-slip.
Finishes	Top layer is sealed when color glaze is baked on.	Unglazed tiles must be sealed to resist stains; they may be waxed. Mexican pavers are very soft and can be sealed.
Relative Cost	Medium to very high.	Medium to high.

Square mosaics, mottled in tones of the same color family, glazed matte surface, set with a deep-toned grout.

Hand-made terra cotta pavers, unglazed, set with a punctuated, though harmonizing, grout.

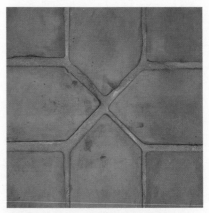

French terra cotta tiles of various sizes and shapes, create a distinct pattern when set together.

Functionally, you will want to consider how the material will be used. If water is likely to get on the floor, the width of any grout lines and the material's surface finish are important. Unglazed quarry tile does not sufficiently resist water or staining for use in a kitchen unless it's sealed. Also, many of these materials are slippery when wet unless their surface is textured to provide traction. Because many of the heavier stone materials are laid in a thick bed of mortar, their installation is usually left to professionals, although such an installation is not beyond the skills of a serious do-it-yourselfer. The preparation and installation chapters of this book will focus on ceramic tile flooring installed over a thin, adhesive bed.

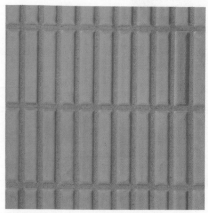

Glazed, narrow rectangular mosaics, pre-glued to backing sheets, set with a harmonizing grout.

Marble	Slate and Other Stone Materials	Brick
12″ to 18″ units. ¼″ to ⅜″ thick. Squares and rectangles are common shapes.	12″ to 24″ squares or rectangles, and irregular or random shapes up to 24″ wide. Large slabs up to 6′ can be ordered.	7″ × 11½″ × 3⅝″ rectangles. Splits available ⁷⁄₁₆″ thick.
Unusual colors and patterns, depending on origin. Glossy or matte finish.	Colors and mottling depend on origin; some have oxide deposits.	Dark red "new" brick, dark red and white mortar-textured "old" brick. Splits come in a wide variety of earth, blue, and green tones.
Should be sealed and polished professionally. May be waxed with a special product.	Most should be sealed for best wear. Sealing darkens slate. Waxing is unnecessary.	Should be sealed. Waxing is unnecessary.
Medium to very high.	Medium to very high.	Low to medium.

Glazed, glossy, smooth-surfaced square tiles of a small scale, set with a semi-contrasting grout.

Rectangular, brick-scale Italian terra cotta tiles, set in a concrete mortar bed, create a visual direction.

Machine-made quarry tiles, unglazed, open textured, set with a monochromatic grout.

CONSIDERING
CARPET FLOORS

With its wide range of colors, fibers, and textures, carpet is one of the most luxurious choices for flooring. Its softness and resilience invite you to sit or stretch out on the floor itself. The higher and denser the pile and thicker the pad, the warmer and quieter it is to walk on. The broad expanse of a carpet creates a simple sweep of color which can provide a quiet visual foundation for the room and at the same time, greet the eye with a delicate play of light and lustre. These qualities have made carpet a favorite choice for almost any room.

When considering carpet, keep in mind the nature of the material as it relates to the room's function. For example, is the room subject to moisture? Because many carpet pad materials, carpet backings, and pile fibers are absorbent, carpet materials can be subject to moisture damage. For installation in kitchens and bathrooms, choose carpet fibers that resist moisture and aren't subject to mildew. If ventilation is also a problem, you may want to consider an alternative material.

By its nature, carpet has a great deal of surface area—the top of a carpet consists only of the tips of the fibers, but the sides of these fibers are also part of a carpet's overall surface. Because of this, carpet fibers catch and hold grit and dirt. These particles will abrade and dull the carpet or even cut off the fibers unless they're regularly removed by vacuuming. For areas of heavy traffic, such as entryways, or areas that are subject to spills and crumbs, such as kitchens, dining rooms, and even family rooms, you will want to consider the maintenance implications of carpet as a flooring option. In some cases you can compensate for these functional considerations by selecting a low and dense carpet pile.

Because carpet has thickness and flexibility and is usually laid over a pad, it can be used on floors that have surface irregularities, essentially hiding or camouflaging them. When other flooring choices might require extensive subfloor preparation, carpeting may be an effective way to transform the room easily.

Below: A quiet basketweave pattern in this neutral gray and white carpet keeps a simple space feeling tailored and calm. *Right:* Plush carpet in a warm creme links one space to the next with an easy three-step transition. The architectural space retains its expansive quality without losing a feeling of quiet elegance, warmth, and comfort.

CARPET FLOORS

When selecting any flooring material, you address a number of design issues. Perhaps the first is the ambient quality of the room and the overall feeling you want it to have. The illustrations below show how carpet can create different effects in the look of the same four room settings shown throughout this chapter.

Carpet gives a broad, expansive, soft look, and offers you a wide range of colors and textures from which to choose. Both of these design features—texture and color—speak with a potentially strong voice, so if your priority is for bold color, choose an even texture. If your priority is a carpet with a lot of texture, choose a quiet color. Bright and vivid colors are enticing on the swatch, but select them with care. They make a forceful statement which can be overwhelming when installed throughout a room, and the color can lose its appeal over time. Neutral colors such as beige, taupe, creme, celadon, and grey are generally a good design solution. They yield a versatile background that does not conflict with the room's overall decorative scheme, and

Carpet in the kitchen adds a softness and warmth that can make the kitchen an inviting, full-range living area for family and friends. A small grid-like pattern of contrasting points of color provides visual interest without drawing undue attention to the floor. Carpet in the kitchen makes sense when soil and spills are infrequent events, and the lower and tighter the pile, the easier it is to maintain this type of material.

Plush, luxurious, uninterrupted color leads the eye through the living room and out to the landscape beyond, signaling expansion, calm, quiet, and comfort. Though gracious and refined, carpet almost serves as a piece of furniture: being a warm, textile material, it invites you to settle down and stretch out.

neutrals can also satisfy the urge for color in the richness of their texture and pile.

To ensure that your carpet installation is both cost-effective and enduringly attractive, carefully plan the layout. You'll want to figure out both the pile direction and the best seam placements. Carpet pile—whether it is looped, cut, or sculptured, has a definite direction, or nap. When you install carpet with the pile leaning toward the main doorway, you get the most lustrous visual effect of color and texture as you enter the room.

If you have to seam carpet, make sure the pile of each piece is oriented in the same direction, so that the visual effect is one of a continuous surface; the seams will be concealed by that continuity. Avoid placing seams in areas that bear heavy traffic. Don't place a seam across a door opening; traffic will eventually take its toll and loosen the seam. Whenever possible, keep seams perpendicular to the largest window openings so they are parallel to the rays of light, and less visible than those that cross the rays.

Soft texture and a single sweep of wall-to-wall color reflect the nature of a bedroom—a peaceful place wrapped in calm and quietude. Furnishings enhance the effect by picking up the same color theme so that all interior treatments work together to shape a unified whole.

Carpet in the bathroom counterbalances the cool edge of typically slick-surfaced fixtures. This flooring approach makes a hard environment softer and more luxurious—even when using low-pile materials in neutral colors. Man-made fibers won't absorb water, which makes carpet a suitable finish for bathroom floors.

CARPET MATERIALS

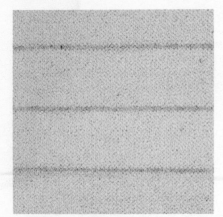

Loop-pile carpet with a narrow stripe gives a definite visual direction to the room in which it is installed.

Woven carpet, with a tiny blue grid over a contrasting background, gives subtle highlights and color variations.

Some fibers age better than others. But then, you may not want to live with the same carpet forever, and this can affect the quality of the carpet you choose. Wool continues to be the best-quality carpet you can buy, but it is also the most expensive. Manufacturers have been steadily improving the quality of man-made fibers over the last 30 years, and there are many beautiful and durable synthetics which are usually less expensive than wool. The characteristics of carpet fibers and how the carpeting is made affect its durability. Consider these other important selection issues:

Weave. Ninety-eight percent of carpet sold is tufted—the yarn is pushed through a primary backing to form loops, and then bonded to a secondary

CARPET MATERIALS

	Wool	Nylon
Resiliency	Excellent. Feels springy underfoot.	Very good. Resists crushing.
Resistance to: Soil	Very good. When soiled may be difficult to clean.	Very good. More easily cleaned than wool.
Abrasion	Very good.	Very good.
Static	Tends to hold static unless treated.	Metal threads almost always included to resist static.
Fading	Direct sunlight will damage fiber over time.	May be damaged by prolonged exposure to sunlight.
Mildew and Pests	Usually treated by the manufacturer to prevent damage.	Fiber naturally resists damage from mildew and pests.
Relative Cost	High.	Medium to high.

Cut-pile carpet, in a larger scaled three-color theme, makes a stronger statement of pattern.

Cut-and-loop pile can create an orderly pattern and subtle texture through the design of the weave itself.

backing. Next most common is woven construction—the yarn itself is woven together like a tapestry to form its own backing. Woven carpet, including Axminster, Wilton, and some velvets, is more expensive than tufted carpet.

Density. Generally the more yarn per square inch, the more durable the carpet.

Twist. High-quality carpet has resilience; it has tightly twisted yarn which readily springs back to its original shape when crushed.

Cost. Quality is almost always directly related to cost—you get what you pay for. In general, carpet costs have not risen as rapidly as those of other types of flooring.

Cut pile, plush and elegant, gives a fresh, soft effect with a continuous sweep of light, bright color.

Polyester	Acrylic	Polypropylene Olefin
Fair. May crush.	Good. Almost as resilient as wool.	Differs depending on type of pile and carpet construction.
Fair. Cleans well.	Good. Must be treated after deep cleaning.	Very good—doesn't hold soil.
Excellent.	Low.	Very good.
Not prone to static.	Will not hold static.	Will not hold static.
Damaged by heat and sunlight.	Good. High color life.	Usually treated to resist fading.
Treated to resist mildew. Not likely to attract pests.	Fiber naturally resists damage from mildew and pests.	Fiber naturally resists damage from mildew and pests.
Low to medium.	Low to medium.	Low.

Loop-pile carpet, lightly salted and peppered with a variety of colors, gives the effect of a neutral tweed.

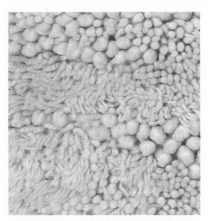

Cut-and-loop pile carpet renders a varied, random pattern using texture as the key design element.

Loop-pile carpet in bands of alternating colors, gives a tailored, clearly defined herringbone look.

PLANNING YOUR PROJECT

Dealing with Professionals

There are many types of professionals who can help you in the planning process. Interior designers are trained to help you make design and selection choices, and it may be well worth your while to purchase even a half an hour of their services. When you have an idea of the material you want, you'll need to decide whether to install the new floor yourself or have it done professionally—in whole or in part.

Before you approach a contractor, dealer, or installer, it's a good idea to do some homework. The more you know about your budget, your existing situation, and what you want your new floor to look like, the easier it will be to gather the information you need and to ask the appropriate questions. Take along a dimensioned drawing of your room or rooms (see pages 36–37).

A dealer or supplier can help you estimate the amount of material you'll need and tell you how much extra to allow for mistakes, damaged pieces, and later repairs. He or she can also help you determine what preparation your existing floor may need, so be sure to describe your existing floor covering, subfloor material, and floor structure (see pages 39–57). Many dealers carry all the tools and supplies necessary for do-it-yourself installation. They will rent or lend these to you. Or they can refer you to an installer if you plan to have the floor installed professionally.

Doing it Yourself

If you're accustomed to doing home improvement projects yourself, you'll want to consider installing your own flooring. In some cases it will save you time and money, although in other cases installation may already be included in the price of materials or may require considerable skill. As a general rule, the less expensive the materials and the higher the labor costs, the greater the savings by doing it yourself. The more expensive the materials or the larger the size of sheet flooring, the higher the cost of errors due to improper installation.

Do-It-Yourself or Professional Installation: Time, Money, and Skill Comparisons

This chart will help you compare the amount of time and money as well as the level of skill required for each type of flooring that's covered. It helps you see what's involved in doing a job yourself, or in having it done professionally. On the facing page you'll find a worksheet to help you itemize the details of your specific project. Use it to help determine the savings and other benefits you gain by doing it yourself.

	Cost of Materials	Cost of Professional Installation	Time Required for Professional Installation	Skills Required for Do-it-Yourself Installation
Wood	Moderate to high.	Relatively high. May include sanding and finishing.	Time consuming.	Basic woodworking. The work is repetitive, so you get better at it as you go along. Special tools speed the process.
Resilient	Low to moderate; can be least expensive material.	Relatively low. Sometimes included in the cost of the material.	Goes quickly.	Installing tiles is easy. For sheet goods, accurate measuring and cutting are needed. Often two people are needed to handle sheet materials without creasing or tearing.
Ceramic Tile, Brick, and Stone	Moderate to high.	Relatively high.	Most time consuming.	Careful layout and accurate tile placement required. Cutting requires special tools.
Carpet	Low to high. Pad is extra.	Relatively low to moderate. Often included in the cost of material.	Goes quickly.	Accurate measuring, cutting, and seaming are needed, and specialized tools. Often two people are needed to handle heavy rolls.

Cost Comparison Worksheet

To work out the details of dealer versus do-it-yourself installation costs for specific flooring materials for a room of a particular size, use the form outlined here. Some of these services, such as removing furniture, can't be expected from an installer, but they can be negotiated and specially arranged.

Contractor or Dealer Charges

1. Sub-floor preparation:

   Materials $ _____

   Labor $ _____

2. Installation:

   Materials $ _____

   Labor $ _____

3. Additional charges:

   Moving heavy furniture $ _____

   Delivery $ _____

   Finishing door openings, trim, etc. $ _____

   Total $ _____

Do-It-Yourself Costs

1. Preparation of subfloor: _____ square feet of plywood or underlayment at $ _____ $ _____

2. Finish flooring materials: _____ square feet or yards at $ _____ $ _____

3. Tools to buy (list): _____ _____ _____ _____ _____ _____ $ _____

   Tools to rent (list): _____ _____ _____ _____ _____ _____ $ _____

4. Supplies: Adhesive $ _____

   Grout or wood fillers $ _____

   Nails or screws $ _____

   Sealers, stains, finishes $ _____

   Tackless strip for carpet $ _____

   Baseboards, thresholds $ _____

   Other $ _____

   _____ $ _____

   _____ $ _____

   _____ $ _____ $ _____

   Total $ _____

Questions to ask the dealer

■ What are the special characteristics of the material?
■ Does the manufacturer guarantee the material?
■ How easy is it to maintain?
■ How long is the wait for delivery?
■ Does the material cost include installation?
■ Are there any hidden costs?
■ Are there any subfloor conditions that must be met before installing this material?
■ How long will it take to install?
■ Is the installation guaranteed?

Questions to ask the installer

■ Will they remove the furniture?
■ Will they charge if they have to remove furniture?
■ Will they measure the space and plan the layout?
■ Will they inspect and clean the subfloor?
■ How long will it take to install the flooring?
■ Will they finish seams, edges, and door openings?
■ Will they clean up?
■ Will they dispose of old floor covering?
■ Will they inspect the completed installation?
■ Will they guarantee the installation?

PLANNING YOUR PROJECT
CONTINUED

Measuring

Whether you have decided to do some or all of the preparation and installation yourself or with professionals, it's a good idea to do your own measuring and to roughly estimate the amount of material you will need. Whatever material you plan to install, you'll find that a dimensioned drawing of the room will be an indispensible tool throughout the planning phase.

■ Use it as an accurate record of the size and shape of the room, closet and door openings, and the exact placement of fixed elements such as cabinetry, chimneys, pipes, and floor furnace registers.

■ Use it as an accurate representation of the room; a flooring materials dealer, installer, or other professional can use this drawing to give you whatever guidance you need.

■ Use it to compute square footages, so that you can make rough estimates of the amount of materials you'll need, and get an idea of the budget required.

■ Use it as a planning and layout aid, a template, so that you get the most coverage possible for your dollar investment, and the best-looking finished floor for your time.

Rooms come in an infinite variety of sizes and shapes. Some consist of four walls only; others have lots of nooks and jogs, built-in cabinets, closets, and other features which you'll want to take into account. The illustrations show you two sample rooms and the measuring principles you would apply in making your drawings. The following pointers show you one method of measuring the area of a room that has built-in fixtures.

■ Take the overall measurements first. Measure the longest dimension of the room, then the widest dimension, and multiply them together. For example, this room is 20 feet long and 14 feet wide (14 feet × 20 feet = 280 square feet).

■ Measure the length of each permanent feature at its base and multiply it by its width. This is the amount of floor area it displaces.

■ Measure the length of each nook, bay, or closet, and multiply it by its width if you plan to continue the flooring material into those areas. This is the amount of additional square footage of flooring material you'll need.

Make a Rough Estimate

To make a rough estimate of the amount of material you'll have to purchase, plan to add a certain percentage to the total square footage of the room. This will insure that you have enough material for details (such

Measuring a Simple Space

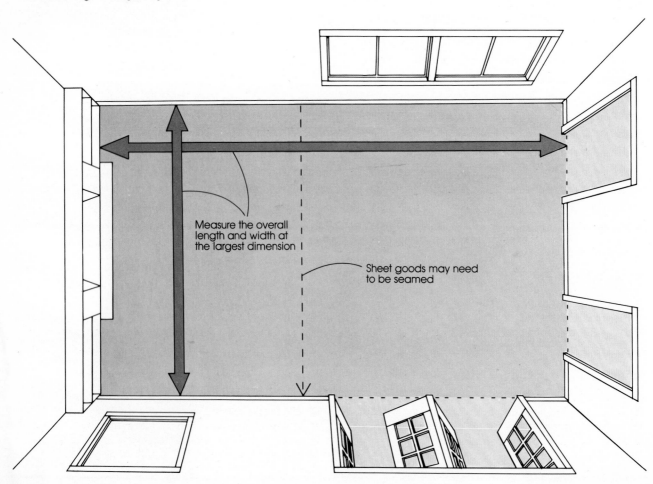

Measure the overall length and width at the largest dimension

Sheet goods may need to be seamed

as extending the flooring into door openings), and will give you an allowance for error and waste. Use the following list to determine how much extra you will need:

Wood strip and plank. This is sold by the square foot; the lumber is available in a variety of lengths, widths, and thicknesses. Add 1-½ square feet for each door opening; 3 percent if the room is fairly regular and rectilinear, and 5 percent if it contains many jogs or nooks.

Wood block and parquet. This is sold by the square foot in boxes. Add 1-½ square feet for each door opening, plus 5 percent for error and wastage.

Resilient and ceramic tile. This is sold by the square foot in boxes. Add 1-½ square feet for each door opening and 5 percent for extra tiles (in case some need to be replaced in the future). Different lots of the same tile may have different tone or color characteristics, so check through the box for consistency.

Resilient sheet and carpet. This is sold by the square yard. You buy it off the roll and have it cut to length. Widths are limited: 6 or 12 feet for resilient sheet, and usually 12 feet for carpet. Add 2 to 4 extra inches to each dimension for a safe cutting margin. If you have to plan for seams (and their placement is crucial), add 8 to 10 percent to your total. If your room has many jogs, nooks or bays, and if you have to take pile direction, seam placements, or pattern matching into consideration, you may have to add as much as 20 percent to your original square footage estimate. Use your dimensioned drawing to consult with your dealer about these allowances.

A Measuring Checklist

■ Use a steel tape—preferably one longer than the greatest length of the room. Over long distances, you'll find it easier if you have a helper hold the end tightly against the surface you're measuring.

■ Measure into doorways to the centerline of the closed door, plus 1 or 2 inches extra.

■ Measure from wall surface to wall surface; either remove baseboards before measuring, or take their thickness into account.

■ Measure every wall in the room—including bays, nooks, jogs, and closets.

■ To keep your sketch accurate in scale and proportion, draw it on a sheet of ¼-inch graph paper and let ¼ inch equal 6 inches or 1 foot. Record the dimensions on your sketch.

Measuring a Room With Built-ins

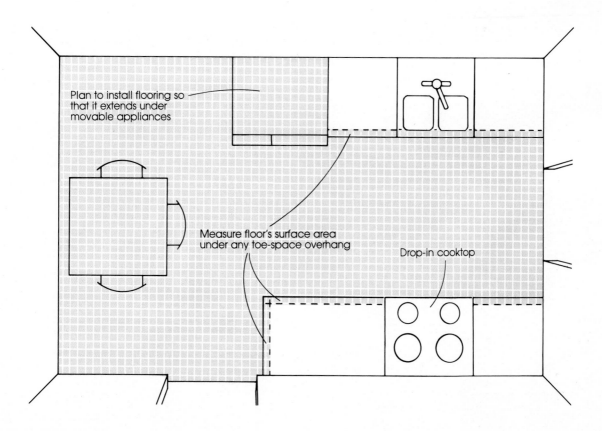

Plan to install flooring so that it extends under movable appliances

Measure floor's surface area under any toe-space overhang

Drop-in cooktop

CHAPTER 2

PREPARATION

Proper preparation of your subfloor is the foundation for an enduringly beautiful finish floor. This chapter shows you how to assess the existing floor structure and tells you what steps to take before the installation begins.

The factors that ensure your floor's lasting beauty begin with selecting the right material, but they certainly don't end there—having a beautiful floor also depends on how well the surface beneath it is prepared. Whether you install the new floor yourself or hire a professional, the preparation phase is critical. The more attention you give to preparation, the greater the success of your finish floor.

Why is preparation so important? Essentially, a finish floor is a relatively thin membrane. Depending on how thick or thin, or how rigid or resilient it is, the finish floor will conform to whatever is beneath it. The subsurface requires careful preparation to make sure that (1) the new floor will be properly supported, (2) its surface will be sufficiently smooth, (3) it will be protected from damage by moisture, (4) it will be able to move with the house, and (5) its level will be at an acceptable height relative to adjacent floor surfaces.

Preparation is also essential because a new flooring material cannot be installed, willy-nilly, over any existing surface. Not all building materials are compatible with each other. Through careful preparation, however, the necessary accommodations can accomplish compatibility. For example, rigid ceramic tile is vulnerable to breakage over a wood subfloor that has an excessive amount of "give." But if you "stiffen" the subfloor with an additional plywood underlayment, you establish compatibility between the two materials.

This chapter is structured to help you think through the preparation process, from start to finish. You may find

Classic materials in a classic design make this marble checkerboard floor enduringly fashionable. Cafe chairs around a marble table, and the richly greened patio beyond, invite you to share in the surrounding life and light.

that preparation is nothing more than confirming that existing flooring conditions are suitable for the installation you want, in which case your next step is to begin installation. On the other hand, you may find that preparation is actually more complex than the installation itself. In either case, understanding the requirements will be worth your time because attention to careful preparation will prevent surprises or problems later on.

The chapter begins by introducing you to the basic structure of a floor, discussing concrete and wood-frame floor systems as they're typically constructed in the United States. This review of a floor's anatomy focuses on how the floor's component parts relate to each other, and how the characteristics of materials used in concrete and wood-frame construction affect a finish floor.

Next is an outline of the preparation steps necessary for installing each type of flooring material: wood, resilient, ceramic, and carpet. Besides describing techniques for handling the material and listing the tools needed for installation, it also tells you what type of subsurface is needed for each material in order to produce a smooth, dry, stable, and durable finish floor. By consulting the accompanying preparation chart for your chosen type of finish floor material, you can quickly find the basic preparation guidelines for the installation of that particular finish floor.

The rest of the chapter details the techniques for various preparation procedures, starting with incidental tasks like removing and trimming down a door or removing baseboard and thresholds. Then it covers techniques for removing various types of existing flooring materials. Finally, it describes how to prepare the subsurface itself—how to make surface repairs, install an underlayment, or even install a wood sleeper subfloor over a concrete slab. With the preparation complete, you will be ready to install your new flooring.

ANATOMY OF A FLOOR

Your finish floor is essentially a "skin" or covering over the real floor of your house—the structural floor that holds up the walls, furnishings, and occupants and keeps out moisture and drafts. Many people never see this structural floor or know how it fits with the other parts of the house. But if you're installing a new finish floor, you must know something about your existing subfloor and framing conditions to avoid covering up problems that may affect your new floor. These two pages show you the anatomy of a concrete slab and a wood-frame subfloor. It is important that you find out which type is underneath your existing finish floor, because the two types are quite different. Each has specific characteristics of material and construction that will affect your new floor.

The illustrations below will help you visualize the floor structure as a series of layers. It is easy to see the importance of some layers; for instance, in wood-frame construction, the foundation and framing layers support the house, and the top layer provides the finished look. But the layer sandwiched in the middle also serves a critical function. This layer is the underlayment, and depending on the materials used for the subfloor and finish floor, it serves one or more of the following purposes: (1) it adds stiffness and rigidity to the floor; (2) it provides a smooth surface for the flooring material; (3) it protects the floor from moisture, drafts, and dust; (4) it increases the floor's resilience; and (5) it provides a suitable surface to which the finish floor can adhere. The discussion of underlayments on page 57 and the charts on pages 43, 44, 46, and 49 will help you decide if your new flooring needs an underlayment, and which material is best. *Note:* The term *underlayment* usually refers to the non-structural material added just before the finish floor is installed, but it is sometimes used to describe the layer immediately below the finish floor—the subfloor or an existing finish floor over which new flooring material will be laid. To avoid confusion, be specific about what you're referring to when you discuss your underlayment or subfloor with a professional.

Concrete Slabs

Concrete is not a waterproof material. It contains a certain amount of moisture for months after it's poured, and it can also wick moisture up from the ground. Therefore, special moisture barriers are often installed beneath the slab before it's poured, to prevent moisture problems which can cause discomfort to you, and deterioration of the finish floor. Because concrete slabs are very strong and stable when properly constructed, they can provide excellent backing for many types of flooring. Rigid materials such as ceramic tiles and wood blocks, as well as flexible materials like resilient and carpet materials, can be glued down to a prepared concrete slab if there is no moisture problem. Laminated wood strip materials are specially manufactured for glued application to concrete slabs, though for traditional wood strip or plank materials, you'll have to construct a wood subfloor over the slab in order to create a subsurface that you can nail into (see page 55).

Anatomy of a Concrete Slab

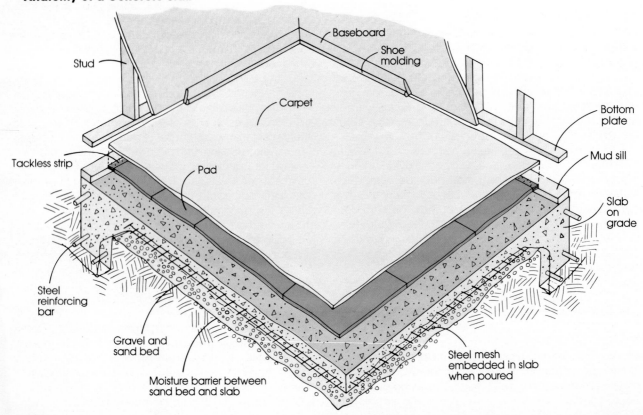

Wood-Frame Subfloors

A wood-frame subfloor has different characteristics. Its separation from the earth protects it from ground moisture, but it is vulnerable to atmospheric humidity and water from spills, plumbing leaks, or roof leaks, which can cause the structure or subfloor to warp or distort from expansion. A wood subfloor is also easy to nail into, and it provides a resilient base for the finish floor.

Structurally, a wood subfloor is only as strong as the foundation and framing beneath it. If the foundation has settled over time, the subfloor might sag; this should be corrected before installing new flooring. If you use very heavy finish floor materials like brick or stone, you may need to reinforce the joist structure to support the additional load. As you can see, the subfloor characteristics, inherent in the structural materials themselves, have important implications for choosing and installing your finish floor. If you need to make structural additions or repairs, refer to Ortho's books, *Basic Carpentry Techniques* and *Basic Remodeling Techniques*.

Anatomy of a Wood-Frame Floor

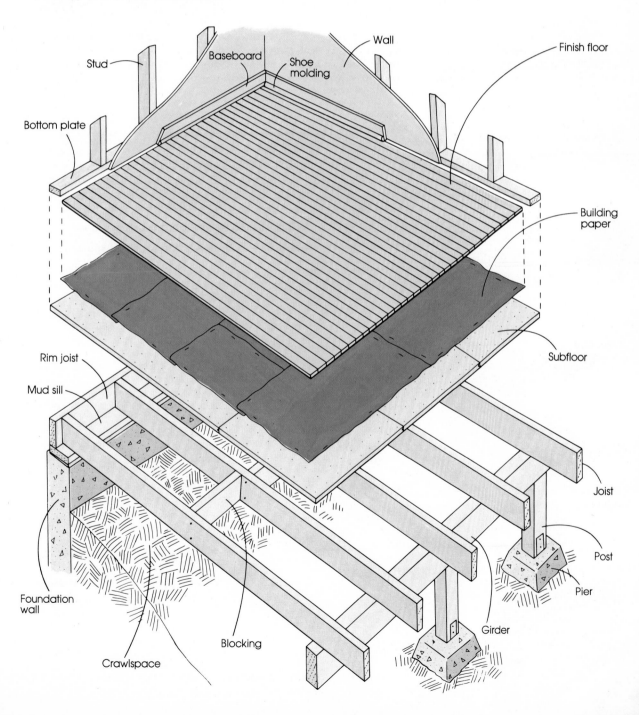

Stud

Baseboard

Shoe molding

Wall

Finish floor

Bottom plate

Building paper

Subfloor

Rim joist

Mud sill

Joist

Post

Pier

Foundation wall

Girder

Blocking

Crawlspace

WOOD FLOORING

Wood flooring will look beautiful and give years of service if it is installed over a properly prepared surface. This means that the subfloor must be structurally sound and the surface for the new floor must be dry, relatively level, smooth, and free of dust or foreign matter. It is very important that any crawlspace or basement area below a wood floor be dry and well ventilated, because wood floors expand from moisture. A concrete slab subfloor must also be free of moisture for the same reason, so that if adhesive is used to glue down the flooring, the bond remains strong and intact.

Preparation Steps

The chart on the facing page summarizes how to install wood floors over existing flooring or subfloors.

In some cases, you may have unique conditions to deal with, such as an extremely humid or dry climate, restrictive floor thickness tolerances, or unusual specifications from the materials manufacturer. Although the chart suggests options where appropriate, you may want to consult a professional or your local building department for recommendations.

In other cases, the chart may indicate that your existing flooring must be removed. When this is done, refer to the chart a second time to see how to prepare the surface that is now exposed.

Storing and Handling Wood Flooring

Wood is responsive to climatic changes, especially excessive humidity (which makes it swell) and excessive heat (which makes it shrink). To keep the wood dry and ready for installation, avoid deliveries during rain or snow. For new construction, plan to have the flooring delivered after the building is closed in and all concrete work, plaster work, and painting are finished.

After delivery, store the material in the room where you plan to install it. Make sure the room is dry and heated to 65 or 70°F. Stack the material log-cabin style, or scatter it around the room so it can acclimate to the environment, for 3 to 5 days.

Tools for Installing Wood Flooring

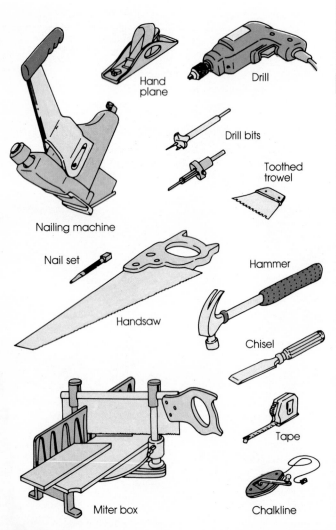

Hand plane

Drill

Drill bits

Toothed trowel

Nailing machine

Nail set

Hammer

Handsaw

Chisel

Miter box

Tape

Chalkline

Nail Schedule

This chart shows the nail sizes and spacing for various wood flooring materials. For planking wider than 4 inches, No. 9 or No. 12 screws are used for additional fastening.

Tongue-and-groove flooring blind-nailed

Flooring	Fastener Size	Spacing
½" × 1½"	1½" machine-driven fastener; 5d screw, cut steel, or wire casing nail.	10" apart
⅜" × 1½"	1¼" machine-driven fastener; 4d bright wire casing nail.	8" apart
¾"	2" machine-driven fastener; 7d or 8d screw or cut nail.	10"–12" apart
¾" × 2¼"	2" machine-driven fastener; 7d or 8d screw or cut nail.	10"–12" apart
¾" × 3¼"	2" machine-driven fastener; 7d or 8d screw or cut nail.	10"–12" apart
¾" × 3" to 8" plank	2" machine-driven fastener; 7d or 8d screw or cut nail.	7"–8" apart into and between joists

(If subfloor is ½" plywood, fasten into each joist, with additional fastening between joists.)

Square-edge flooring face-nailed

⁵⁄₁₆" × 1⅓"	1" 15-gauge fully barbed flooring brad.	1 nail every 5" on alternate sides of strip
⁵⁄₁₆" × 1½"	1" 15-gauge fully barbed flooring brad.	2 nails every 7"
⁵⁄₁₆" × 2"	1" 15-gauge fully barbed flooring brad.	2 nails every 7"

Source: National Oak Flooring Manufacturers Association.

Preparation Steps for Wood Flooring Installations

This chart summarizes the preparation steps required for installing wood flooring materials over various existing floors and floor systems. It assumes that your existing floor structure is in good condition and that any moisture problems are corrected. Specific preparation guidelines and techniques are detailed in this chapter.

Existing Floor	Preparation for Wood Strip and Plank	Preparation for Wood Block and Parquet
Exposed joists	■ Install ¾" T&G CDX plywood subfloor. ■ Lay building paper.	■ Install ¾" T&G CDX/PTS plywood.
Bare concrete	■ Install wood sleeper subfloor. ■ Lay building paper.	■ Remove any sealer or surface finishes. ■ Make surface repairs to slab as needed. ■ Roughen surface for best adhesion.
Wood subfloor **Over wood-frame**	■ Make surface repairs to subfloor as needed. ■ Lay building paper.	■ Make surface repairs to subfloor as needed. ■ If subfloor is very rough or uneven, or has gaps between boards, install ¼"–½" underlayment-grade plywood.
Over concrete slab	■ Make surface repairs to wood subfloor as needed. ■ Lay building paper.	■ Make surface repairs to wood subfloor as needed.
Wood finish floor **Over wood-frame**	■ Make surface repairs to existing floor as needed.	■ If finish flooring boards are not wider than 4", make surface repairs. Remove all surface finish. ■ If boards are wider than 4", install ¼"–½" underlayment-grade plywood.
Over concrete slab	■ Make surface repairs to existing floor as needed.	■ If finish flooring boards are not wider than 4", make surface repairs. Remove all surface finish. ■ If boards are wider than 4", install ¼"–½" underlayment-grade plywood.
Resilient sheet or tile **Over wood-frame**	■ If resilient is cushioned, springy, or not tightly bonded, remove it and make surface repairs as needed. ■ Otherwise, make surface repairs to existing flooring as needed.	■ If resilient is cushioned, springy, or not tightly bonded, remove it and make surface repairs as needed. ■ Otherwise, install ¼" underlayment-grade plywood after making surface repairs as needed.
Over concrete slab	■ Install wood sleeper subfloor. ■ Lay building paper.	■ If resilient is cushioned, springy, or not tightly bonded, remove it and make surface repairs as needed. ■ Remove any sealer or surface finish and roughen surface for best adhesion.
Ceramic tile **Over wood-frame**	■ Remove existing ceramic tile. ■ Make surface repairs as needed. ■ Lay building paper.	■ If tile surface is smooth, flat, and tightly bonded, remove any wax or sealer and grind off surface sheen with a floor sander. Otherwise, remove ceramic tile. ■ Install ¼" underlayment-grade plywood after making surface repairs as needed.
Over concrete slab	■ Install wood sleeper subfloor. ■ Lay building paper.	■ If tile surface is smooth, flat, and tightly bonded, remove any wax or sealer and grind off surface sheen with a floor sander. Otherwise, remove ceramic tile. ■ Make surface repairs to slab as needed. ■ Remove sealer or surface finish; roughen surface.
Carpet **Over wood-frame**	■ Remove existing carpet. ■ Make surface repairs to exposed subfloor as needed. ■ Lay building paper.	■ Remove existing carpet. ■ Make surface repairs to exposed subfloor as needed.
Over concrete slab	■ Remove existing carpet. ■ Install wood sleeper subfloor. ■ Lay building paper.	■ Remove existing carpet. ■ Make surface repairs to exposed slab as needed. ■ Remove sealer or surface finish; roughen surface.

RESILIENT FLOORING

Resilient materials are manufactured in light gauges, and because they have no inherent structural strength, they will conform to the surface on which they are laid. Subfloor cracks, plywood voids, or even small depressions from nailheads will potentially show through the finish floor. This occurrence diminishes the smooth visual continuity of a resilient floor, and makes it subject to uneven wear, which reduces its durability. If the subfloor or the existing floor is not perfectly smooth, install a new underlayment before laying the resilient flooring.

Resilient materials also need to be installed over surfaces that are entirely free of moisture. Whereas small amounts of subsurface moisture may evaporate harmlessly through other flooring materials, such as wood or carpet, a resilient floor acts as a moisture barrier. Moisture that collects underneath resilient flooring can force up the adhesive bond. In humid climates, choose a waterproof and stable underlayment material.

Handling Resilient Sheet Flooring

Unroll sheet flooring in the room where it will be installed or in a room heated to 70°F for at least 24 hours before installation; it needs to "relax." When ready to install, reroll with the face side in.

Preparation Steps

The chart summarizes what steps you'll need to take for installing resilient floors over existing flooring materials or subfloors. It assumes that your existing floor is in good condition and that any moisture problems have been corrected.

In some cases, you may have unique conditions to deal with, such as an extremely humid climate, or unusual installation specifications from the materials manufacturer.

In other cases, the chart may indicate that your existing flooring must be removed. When you have accomplished this step, refer to the chart a second time to see what needs to be done to prepare the surface that is now exposed.

Preparation Steps for Resilient Sheet and Tile

This chart summarizes the preparation steps required for installing resilient flooring materials over various existing floors and floor systems.

Existing Floor	Preparation for Resilient Sheet or Tile
Exposed joists	■ Install ¾" T&G CDX plywood subfloor. ■ Install ¼"–½" particle-board underlayment, or underlayment-grade plywood. ■ Fill joints and underlayment nail- or screw-head depressions, and sand surface smooth.
Bare concrete	■ Make surface repairs to slab as needed.
Wood floor or subfloor Over wood-frame	■ Make surface repairs as needed. ■ Install ¼"–½" particle-board underlayment, or underlayment-grade plywood. ■ Fill joints and underlayment nail- or screw-head depressions, and sand surface smooth.
Over concrete slab	■ Remove all wood materials to expose the concrete. ■ Make surface repairs to the slab as needed.
Resilient sheet or tile Over wood-frame	■ If existing resilient is cushioned or springy, remove it and make surface repairs as needed. ■ If existing resilient is embossed, not tightly bonded, or has wax or surface sheen, install ¼" particle-board underlayment, or underlayment-grade plywood. ■ Fill joints and underlayment nail- or screw-head depressions, and sand surface smooth.
Over concrete slab	■ If existing resilient is cushioned or springy, or not tightly bonded, remove it and make surface repairs to exposed concrete as needed. ■ If embossed, smooth the surface with a liquid-type underlayment. Otherwise, remove wax and roughen the surface.
Ceramic tile Over wood-frame	■ If possible, remove existing tile; otherwise, smooth and even out the surface with a liquid-type underlayment. ■ After removing existing ceramic tile, make surface repairs to exposed subfloor as needed. ■ If subfloor is very rough, install ¼"–½" particle-board underlayment, or underlayment-grade plywood. Fill joints and underlayment nail- or screw-head depressions, and sand surface smooth.
Over concrete slab	■ If possible, remove existing tile; otherwise, smooth and even out the surface with a liquid-type underlayment. ■ After removing existing ceramic tile, make surface repairs to exposed slab as needed. If surface is very rough or uneven, smooth it with a liquid-type underlayment.
Carpet Over wood-frame	■ Remove existing carpet. ■ Make surface repairs to exposed subfloor as needed. ■ If subfloor is very rough, install ¼"–½" particle-board underlayment, or underlayment-grade plywood. Fill joints and underlayment nail- or screw-head depressions, and sand surface smooth.
Over concrete slab	■ Remove existing carpet. ■ Make surface repairs to exposed slab as needed.

Adhesives for Resilient Flooring

Different adhesives are used for different types of flooring materials and subfloor situations. They are classified according to the types listed below. Follow the manufacturer's instructions carefully, and use caution with flammable adhesives. The room should always be well ventilated, with no pilot lights on. Avoid using equipment with electric motors that may cause sparks, and do not smoke.

Adhesive	Flooring Material	Subfloor	Comments
Water-soluble paste	Vinyl materials with rubber backing, cork, vinyl cork (not solid vinyl, asphalt, vinyl-composition).	Concrete or wood-frame above grade.	Must be rolled.
Asphalt-based (asphalt emulsion, cut-back asphalt)	Asphalt, vinyl-composition.	Concrete or wood above or below grade.	Do not mix with water for on- or below-grade floors.
Latex adhesive	Solid vinyl, vinyl-composition, rubber, cork, linoleum.	Concrete or wood above, on, or below grade.	Good for moisture situations, dries quickly. Keep from freezing; wear rubber gloves.
Alcohol-resin	Vinyl, rubber, cork, linoleum.	Concrete or wood above grade.	Not entirely waterproof.
Epoxy cement	Solid vinyl, rubber tiles.	Concrete or wood above, on, or below grade.	Good for perimeter and seam sealing, high strength, must be mixed. Wear rubber gloves; provide ventilation.
Cove base cement (solvent-based)	Vinyl and rubber cove base.	Above grade.	Combustible. Wear rubber gloves; provide ventilation.
Synthetic rubber cement	Vinyl cove base, metal nosings and edges (not asphalt, vinyl-composition).	Any wall.	Provide ventilation.
Neoprene adhesive	Vinyl and rubber stair treads, nosings, corner guards.	Any wall.	Water resistant. Provide ventilation.

Tools for Installing Resilient Flooring

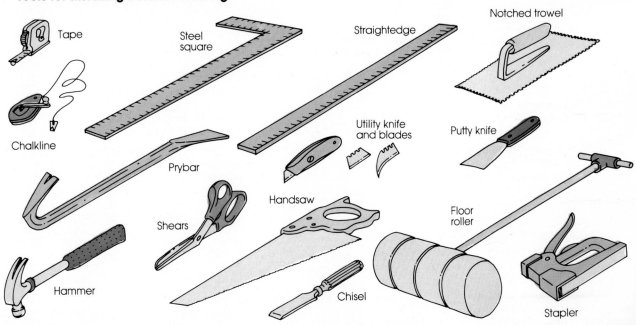

Tape · Steel square · Straightedge · Notched trowel · Chalkline · Prybar · Utility knife and blades · Putty knife · Shears · Handsaw · Floor roller · Hammer · Chisel · Stapler

Ceramic tile and masonry are durable materials that can last for centuries, but a tile floor is only as sound as the substructure beneath it.

Masonry, which includes floor tile, brick, stone, terrazzo, and pavers, creates a heavy floor. If the weight of the masonry is greater than the subfloor structure was designed to bear, you may need to have a mortar bed installed or to make structural changes before installing these heavier materials.

Wood subfloor structures have a certain amount of "give" or springiness. This can cause a tile floor to crack at the grout lines or across individual tiles. To prevent that, double wood subfloors (consisting of plywood nailed over the existing, well-fastened subfloor) are recommended when you are installing tiles in a home that has a wood-frame substructure.

Because a concrete slab—particularly older concrete that has cured for some time—is a rigid surface that has no give, it makes an excellent base for setting tile or masonry flooring. But be sure that there are no crumbly patches or areas where aggregate is exposed.

Preparation Steps

The chart on this page summarizes what steps you'll need to take for installing ceramic tile floors over existing flooring materials or subfloors. It assumes that your existing floor is in good condition and that any moisture problems are corrected. It tells you what steps to take in most common situations.

In some cases, you may have unique conditions to deal with, such as unusual installation specifications from the materials manufacturer. Although the chart suggests options where appropriate, if you have any questions, you may want to consult a professional or your local building department for special conditions and recommendations.

In other cases, the chart may indicate that your existing flooring must be removed. When you have accomplished this step, refer to the chart a second time to see what needs to be done to prepare the surface that is now exposed.

Preparation Steps for Ceramic Tile Installations

This chart summarizes the preparation steps required for installing ceramic tile materials over various existing floors.

Existing Floor	Preparation for Ceramic Tile
Exposed joists	■ Install a double-wood subfloor: First install ⅝" T&G CDX plywood directly over the joists. Then install exterior-grade plywood over the subfloor. Use ⅜" CDX/PTS plywood for organic adhesives or ⅝" for epoxies.
Bare concrete	■ Make surface repairs to concrete as needed. ■ Roughen the surface for best adhesion.
Wood subfloor Over wood-frame	■ Make surface repairs to subfloor as needed. ■ Install CDX/PTS plywood, using ⅜" for organic adhesives, or ⅝" for epoxies.
Over concrete slab	■ Remove all wood materials to expose the slab. ■ Make surface repairs to concrete as needed. ■ Roughen the surface for best adhesion.
Wood finish floor Over wood-frame	■ Remove finish flooring to expose the subfloor. ■ Install ⅜" CDX/PTS plywood for organic adhesives, or ⅝" for epoxies.
Over concrete slab	■ Remove all wood materials to expose the slab. ■ Make surface repairs to concrete as needed. ■ Roughen the surface for best adhesion.
Resilient sheet and tile Over wood-frame	■ If the resilient flooring was installed over particleboard underlayment, remove both. ■ If the resilient material is installed over plywood, is dense (neither cushioned nor springy), and is sound, remove wax or finish and roughen the surface. Otherwise, remove the flooring to expose the subfloor. ■ Install exterior-grade plywood over the subfloor; use ⅜" CDX/PTS or organic adhesives, or ⅝" for epoxies.
Over concrete slab	■ If resilient material is cushioned, springy, or unsound, remove it and repair exposed slab as needed. ■ Otherwise, remove wax or finish and roughen the surface, select an adhesive that is compatible with the existing resilient material.
Ceramic tile Over wood-frame	■ If possible, remove existing tile, exposing the subfloor. Otherwise, secure loose tiles, and roughen the surface for best adhesion. If surface is uneven, smooth it with a liquid-type underlayment. New tile can be glued down directly with appropriate adhesive. ■ If existing tile can be removed, install exterior-grade plywood over the subfloor. Use ⅜" CDX/PTS for organic adhesives, or ⅝" for epoxies.
Over concrete slab	■ If possible, remove existing tile, exposing the slab. Otherwise, secure loose tiles, and roughen the surface for best adhesion. If surface is uneven, smooth it with a liquid-type underlayment. New tile can be glued down directly with appropriate adhesive. ■ If existing tile can be removed, make surface repairs to exposed slab as needed.
Carpet Over wood-frame	■ Remove existing carpet to expose subfloor. ■ Install exterior-grade plywood over the subfloor, using ⅜" CDX/PTS for organic adhesives, or ⅝" for epoxies.
Over concrete slab	■ Remove existing carpet to expose slab. ■ Make surface repairs to exposed concrete as needed.

Tools for Installing Ceramic Tile

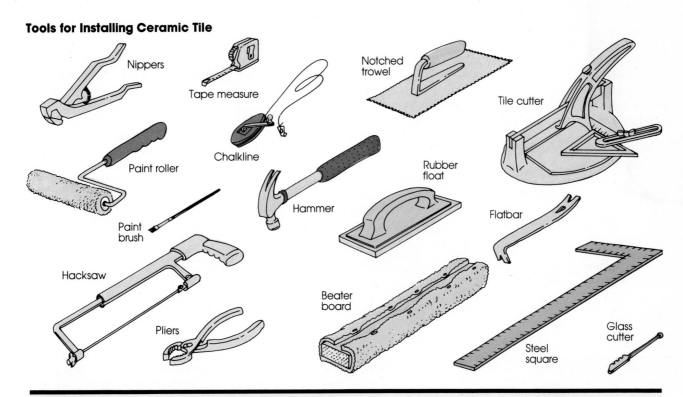

Nippers · Tape measure · Notched trowel · Tile cutter · Chalkline · Paint roller · Rubber float · Hammer · Paint brush · Flatbar · Hacksaw · Beater board · Steel square · Glass cutter · Pliers

Adhesives and Mortars for Tile Floors

This chart offers an overview of the different types of adhesives and mortars that are used for ceramic tile installations. Consult with your tile dealer about the specific conditions of your own installation. Use these recommendations along with the manufacturer's specifications to help you select the right adhesive.

Adhesives and Mortars	Composition	Conditions for Use	Comments
Type I mastic	Solvent based.	For damp areas.	Thin-set, ready to use, flammable, may irritate skin and lungs.
Type II mastic	Latex based.	For dry areas only.	Easy to clean up, nonflammable.
Dry-set mortar	Portland cement mixed with sand, additives, and water.	For concrete or glass-mesh mortarboard. Not recommended for use over wood or resilient floors.	Not water-resistant, nonflammable, easy to clean up, rigid, impact-resistant.
Latex-portland cement mortar	Portland cement mixed with sand and liquid latex, sometimes diluted with water.	For concrete or glass-mesh mortarboard, not recommended for use over wood or resilient floors.	More water-resistant than dry-set mortar and easier to work with, less rigid, tends to move.
Epoxy adhesive	Epoxy resin mixed with hardener.	Preferred adhesive for moisture-prone areas. Use over plywood or old resilient.	Expensive, toxic to skin, works best between 70–85°F.
Epoxy mortar	Epoxy resin mixed with hardener, sand, and portland cement.	Preferred adhesive for moisture-prone areas. Use over concrete or existing ceramic tile.	More body than adhesive. More chemical resistance than adhesive; levels uneven subsurfaces.
Portland cement mortar	Traditional mortar bed—portland cement mixed with sand and water.	Preferred adhesive for moisture-prone areas or where subfloor is uneven.	Thick bed (¾" to 1¼"), reinforced with wire mesh, long-lasting, waterproof, offers structural strength, requires careful installation.

CARPET

Except for cushion-backed carpet or very thin goods, carpet can conceal defects and irregularities in the sub-surface quite well; the thicker the pad or carpet, the greater its success. In general, carpet installations require very little preparation. But in all instances, the subfloor surface must be dry, free of debris, and essentially smooth. If you are replacing an existing carpet, you can reuse the existing pad and tackless strip if they are in good condition.

Concrete slab subfloors with radiant heat pipes deserve special consideration. If you intend to nail down tackless strip (see page 84) you run the risk of puncturing a pipe. To locate the pipes, moisten the slab around the perimeter of the room wherever you intend to nail down tackless strip, then turn up the heat. Watch for areas that dry first, and mark them with chalk. These are the spots to avoid when nailing.

Preparation Steps

The chart on the facing page summarizes what steps you'll need to take for installing carpet over existing flooring materials or subfloors. It assumes that your existing floor is in good condition and that any moisture problems are corrected. It tells you what steps to take in most common situations.

In some cases, you may have unique conditions to deal with, such as unusual installation specifications from the materials manufacturer. Although the chart suggests options where appropriate, you may want to consult a local professional or your local building department for special conditions and recommendations.

In other cases, the chart may indicate that your existing flooring must be removed. When you have accomplished this step, refer to the chart a second time to see what

needs to be done to prepare the flooring surface that is now exposed.

Storing and Handling Carpet

Store carpet on a clean surface in a dry area. If the surface is damp, lay a sheet of plastic underneath the carpet roll. In order to rough-cut the material to size, plan to cut pieces off the roll in a clean, dry, large, open area such as a large room or even the driveway or basement. Then carry the pieces separately into the rooms where they will be installed. In general, roll and unroll carpet pieces in the direction the pile naturally leans.

Carpet is awkward to handle because of its weight and bulk; you may need a helper. One good way to handle a large unrolled piece of carpet for carrying is to fold both long sides toward the center and then loosely roll it up. The shorter roll is bulky, but easier to maneuver.

Tools for Installing Carpet

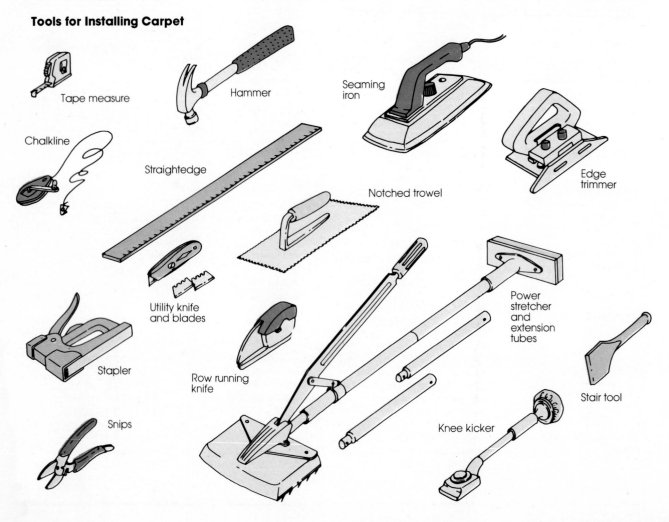

Tape measure · Hammer · Seaming iron · Chalkline · Straightedge · Notched trowel · Edge trimmer · Utility knife and blades · Stapler · Row running knife · Power stretcher and extension tubes · Stair tool · Snips · Knee kicker

Preparation Steps for Carpet Installations

This chart summarizes the preparation steps required for installing carpet over various existing floors and floor systems. For additional guidelines on how to use the chart, see "Preparation Steps" on the facing page.

Existing Floor	Preparation for Conventional Carpet	Preparation for Cushion-Backed Carpet
Exposed joists	■ Install ¾" T&G CDX plywood subfloor. If carpet is thin, fill joints and surface depressions and sand smooth, or use CDX/PTS plywood.	■ Install ¾" T&G CDX/PTS plywood subfloor. Fill joints and surface depressions and sand smooth.
Bare concrete	■ Make surface repairs as needed.	■ Make surface repairs to slab as needed.
Wood subfloor **Over wood-frame**	■ Make surface repairs to subfloor as needed. ■ If subfloor is very rough, uneven, or has gaps between boards, install ¼"–½" underlayment-grade plywood.	■ Make surface repairs to subfloor as needed. If subfloor is very rough, uneven, or has gaps between boards, install ¼"–½" underlayment-grade plywood. ■ Fill joints and surface depressions and sand smooth.
Over concrete slab	■ Remove all wood materials to expose the slab. ■ Make surface repairs as needed.	■ Remove all wood materials to expose the slab. ■ Make surface repairs to slab as needed.
Wood finish floor **Over wood-frame**	■ Make surface repairs to existing floor as needed.	■ Make surface repairs to existing floor as needed. ■ Install ¼"–½" underlayment-grade plywood. ■ Fill joints and surface depressions and sand smooth.
Over concrete slab	■ Remove all wood materials to expose the slab. ■ Make surface repairs to concrete.	■ Remove all wood materials to expose the slab. ■ Make surface repairs to concrete as needed.
Resilient sheet or tile **Over wood-frame**	■ Make surface repairs to existing flooring as needed.	■ Make surface repairs to existing flooring as needed. ■ If resilient is smooth and tightly bonded, remove wax, and roughen surface for best adhesion. ■ If resilient is not well bonded, remove it. ■ Install ¼"–½" underlayment-grade plywood. ■ Fill joints and surface depressions and sand smooth.
Over concrete slab	■ Make surface repairs to existing flooring as needed.	■ Make surface repairs to existing flooring as needed. ■ If resilient is smooth and tightly bonded, remove wax, and roughen surface for best adhesion. ■ If resilient is not well bonded, remove it. ■ Install ¼"–½" underlayment-grade plywood. ■ Fill joints and surface depressions and sand smooth.
Ceramic tile **Over wood-frame**	■ If possible, remove existing tile. If not, make surface repairs. To smooth and even out the tile surface, use a liquid-type underlayment.	■ If possible, remove existing tile. ■ If not, make surface repairs. To smooth and even out the tile surface, use a liquid-type underlayment, compatible with the carpet adhesive.
Over concrete slab	■ If tile is smooth and tightly bonded, even out the tile surface with a liquid-type underlayment. ■ Otherwise, remove it, or make surface repairs as needed.	■ If possible, remove existing ceramic tile. ■ Otherwise, make surface repairs as needed to the existing flooring. To smooth and even out the tile surface, use a liquid-type underlayment, compatible with the carpet adhesive.
Carpet **Over wood-frame**	■ Remove existing carpet. ■ Make surface repairs to subfloor as needed. ■ If subfloor is very rough, uneven, or has gaps between boards, install ¼"–½" underlayment-grade plywood.	■ Remove existing carpet. ■ Make surface repairs to subfloor as needed. ■ If subfloor is very rough, uneven, or has gaps between boards, install ¼"–½" underlayment-grade plywood. ■ Fill joints and surface depressions and sand smooth.
Over concrete slab	■ Remove existing carpet. ■ Make surface repairs.	■ Remove existing carpet. ■ Make surface repairs to exposed slab as needed.

GETTING THE ROOM READY

To prepare a room for a new flooring installation, you may have to mark doors to trim them down or remove doors and baseboard. The illustrations on these two pages show you how.

Marking a Door

To trim the bottom of a door, measure up from the existing floor a distance equal to the added flooring height plus ⅛–¼ inch. Mark this trimline position on the hinge pin side of the door.

Removing a Door

Remove doors that will get in the way during the installation process. If you need to trim the door because the new material will increase the height of the floor, measure and mark the trimline first (see the illustration be-low). To knock the hinge pins out, tap them from below with a hammer and 16-penny nail. If there is no access hole in the hinge barrel, place an old screwdriver or dull chisel against the head of the pin and tap it up with a hammer.

Trimming a Door

To trim, lay the door on sawhorses with the marked side up. Holding a straightedge parallel with the door's bottom, mark the cutting line. Cover the line with a piece of masking tape—one on each face of the door—to prevent the saw from splintering the wood. Then redraw the line on the tape. Clamp a straight board securely to the door to guide the saw's shoe, and make the cut with a circular saw.

Marking a Door

Removing a Door

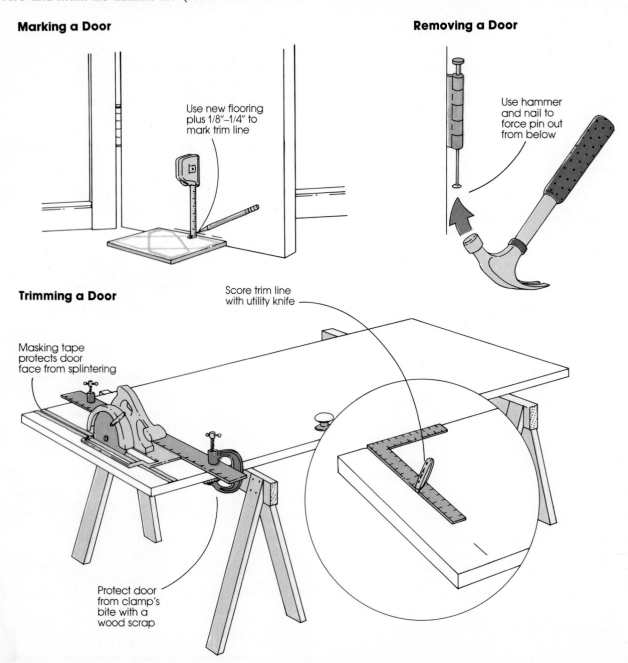

Use new flooring plus 1/8"–1/4" to mark trim line

Use hammer and nail to force pin out from below

Trimming a Door

Score trim line with utility knife

Masking tape protects door face from splintering

Protect door from clamp's bite with a wood scrap

Removing Thresholds

Remove thresholds by prying them up from the floor with a metal pry-bar. If the door jambs were undercut to house the threshold, saw the threshold into two pieces and remove each piece separately.

Undercutting Door Trim and Casings

Door trim and casings need not be removed; they can be undercut to allow the new flooring to slip neatly underneath. To do this, lay a piece of new flooring next to the casing, and mark the thickness on the casing. Saw away the casing using a fine-toothed hand saw. Because the saw blade's kerf—the amount of material the teeth remove—will raise the height of the cut if you saw directly on the line, "save the line" by cutting just below it.

Removing Wood Baseboards

To remove wood baseboards, hold a thin scrap of wood against the wall, wedge a prybar between it and the top of the baseboard, and gently coax the baseboard away. If the baseboard starts to pull paint off as it separates from the wall, run a utility knife along the joint before prying the rest of the board away. Work your way along the wall, prying at those points where the baseboard is nailed. If you plan to reinstall the baseboard after the floor is laid, number each section as you remove it.

Removing a Vinyl Cove Base

To remove a vinyl cove base, just loosen it from the wall with a wide-blade putty knife, and strip it away. Scrape the wall with the putty knife to remove any remaining adhesive.

Removing Ceramic Tile Base Borders

To remove ceramic tile base borders, pop each one loose from the wall using a metal prybar. If you are concerned about scratching or damaging your wall, place a scrap of wood behind the bar. Scrape the wall free of any remaining grout or adhesive.

Removing wood thresholds

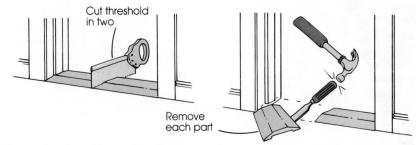

Cut threshold in two

Remove each part

Removing door trim and casings

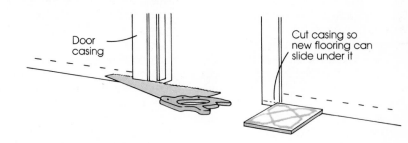

Door casing

Cut casing so new flooring can slide under it

Removing wood baseboard

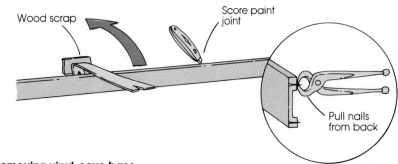

Wood scrap

Score paint joint

Pull nails from back

Removing vinyl cove base

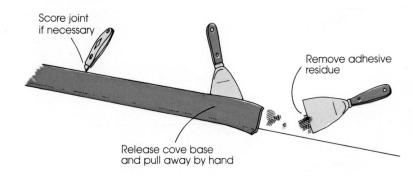

Score joint if necessary

Remove adhesive residue

Release cove base and pull away by hand

Removing ceramic tile

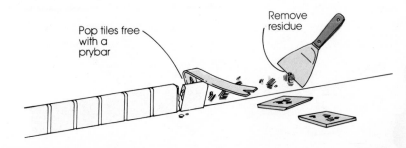

Pop tiles free with a prybar

Remove residue

REMOVING EXISTING FLOORING

For some flooring installations, you will want to pull up an existing finish floor before installing the new material (see charts on pages 43–49). In all cases, use care in removing old flooring. Some materials, such as broken ceramic tiles, are sharp; others, like carpet or wood, have numerous staples or nails. Also, despite frequent cleaning, floors attract years of household dust and grime, so wear gloves and a dust mask for protection. Finally, so that you won't have to repair them later, avoid damaging walls, baseboards, or the subfloor as you remove the existing flooring material.

Removing Wood Flooring

Most wood strip flooring is nailed down and can be pried up with a curved wrecking bar or flat bar. Before prying up plank flooring, bore out any plugs and remove the screws used for additional fastening.

Then, remove any moldings and/or baseboards. Insert a prybar under the first floorboard and force it up. If there is not enough room for the prybar, cut out a section of the first board with a circular saw. Set its blade depth to cut through the finish flooring only—not into the subfloor below. Remove the cut section; then insert the prybar into the opening and pry up the rest of the board.

Proceed across the floor, prying up one board at a time. Work down the length of each board, placing the bar directly under the blind-nailing positions.

If the wood flooring has been glued down, remove it by placing a chisel or prybar against the bottom of each piece and tapping with a hammer to pop the flooring loose, piece by piece.

Removing Resilient Flooring

If the sheet flooring is stapled or glued only around the room's edges, pry up the staples or loosen the glued sheet with a wide putty knife or floor scraper. Roll it up and haul it out of the room. If the sheet was glued down all over, first cut it into 12- or 24-inch strips. Then work each strip free as described above. To pop off individual loose tiles, use a prybar or putty knife. Heat tightly bonded tiles with an iron and then pry up. To remove any remaining adhesive, use a floor scraper or putty knife, or dissolve the residue with hot soapy water, or acetone, mineral spirits, or a similar commercial product. In some localities you can rent a floor stripping machine for removing resilient flooring.

If you have difficulty removing the flooring, consider taking up the underlayment as well. Use a circular saw to cut the floor into 4-foot by 4-foot sections. Set the blade depth to the thickness of the sheet, plus the thickness of the underlayment. You will probably cut through nails, so use an old or disposable blade and wear eye protectors and a respirator. Pry up each section of flooring and underlayment together, and remove. *Note:* Existing resilient flooring may contain asbestos fibers, which are harmful if inhaled. They are embedded in the material, but could be released if you sand, cut, or break it.

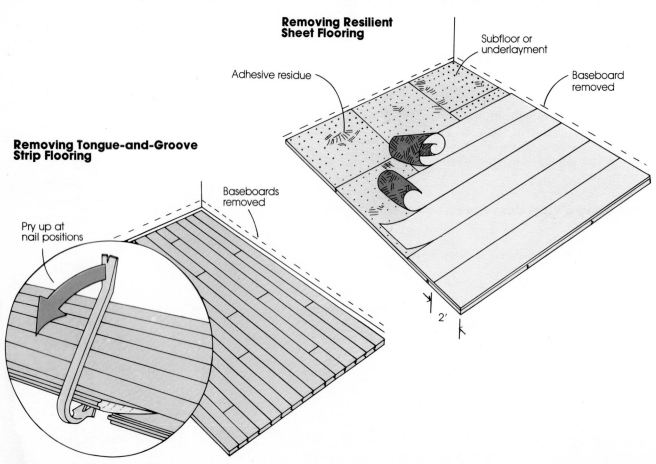

Removing Resilient Sheet Flooring

Adhesive residue

Subfloor or underlayment

Baseboard removed

2'

Removing Tongue-and-Groove Strip Flooring

Baseboards removed

Pry up at nail positions

Removing Ceramic and Masonry Tiles

To remove mastic installations, use a hammer and cold chisel to chip out the grout around one tile. Break the tile with a hammer and remove the pieces. Then position the cold chisel under adjacent tile edges, tap to loosen, and remove them one by one. Scrape any remaining adhesive from the subfloor.

To remove mortar-bed installations, it is generally easier to force up the mortar bed itself than to break the tiles away from it. Insert a large wrecking bar or pick-axe under one corner of the mortar bed and pry it up from the subfloor. Use a sledgehammer to break the bed into sections, and wire cutters or snips to cut the reinforcing mesh embedded in the mortar. Remember that carefully aimed taps are more effective than indiscriminant blows. Avoid excessive force and wear protective goggles and clothing.

Removing Carpet

To remove carpet installed on tackless strip, remove all metal edgings and cut the carpet into 1- or 2-foot-wide bands with a utility knife. Using a screwdriver or prybar, pry up one carpet corner and pull it free from the strip along both walls. Release all the bands in the same way. If you want to keep the carpet in one piece, release one corner and work your way around all the walls.

To remove carpet installed with carpet tacks, slide a flat prybar under one edge of the carpet and pry up several tacks. Then tug hard and pull up the entire carpet, tacks and all. If that doesn't work, loosen each tack with a prybar. Roll up the carpet and haul it away.

To remove stapled pads, tear away whatever you can, pull up the remaining small pieces, and pry up staples from the subfloor with a screwdriver or pliers. Remove the tackless strip with a prybar.

To remove cushion-backed carpet which has been glued down, cut it into 12-inch-wide bands. Use a wide putty knife to work each band free from the subsurface, as you pull them up. Scrape off any remaining chunks of foam and adhesive. If the floor must be smooth, sand off the residue with a rented floor sander, or install an underlayment (see page 57).

Removing Ceramic Tile

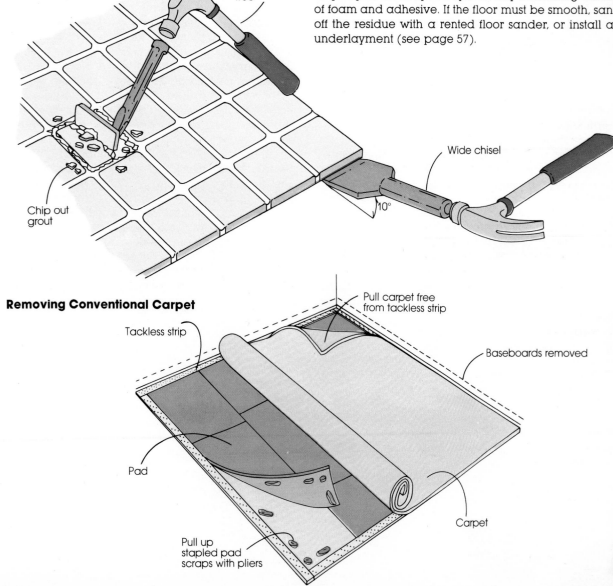

Tap pieces free

Chip out grout

Wide chisel

10°

Removing Conventional Carpet

Pull carpet free from tackless strip

Tackless strip

Baseboards removed

Pad

Carpet

Pull up stapled pad scraps with pliers

PREPARING A CONCRETE SLAB

To install new flooring over a concrete slab, see the preparation guidelines indicated on the charts on pages 43, 44, 46, and 49. In many instances, you may have to make some basic surface repairs to insure that there is an appropriately clean, smooth, even, and bondable surface for the new flooring.

Remove grease, oil, paint, and dirt. To install any flooring directly on concrete, remove grease, oil, paint flakes, and dirt by scrubbing the surface well with a solution of trisodium phosphate and hot water, or use a special concrete degreasing agent available at most hardware stores. Rinse with clear water and let the floor dry thoroughly.

Fill cracks or holes. If the floor has minor cracks or holes—entry points for water—but is otherwise sound, widen and clean them out. Then fill the cracks or holes with a quick-setting hydraulic cement.

Correct low and high spots. To locate low spots which need to be filled and high spots which need to be leveled, roll a long straight pipe across the slab and watch for gaps between it and the pipe. Fill depressions with patching compound, feathering (smoothing) the filler in to the surrounding floor. To correct high spots, grind them down with a carborundum rubbing stone ("rottenstone"). If extensive smoothing is required, rent a concrete grinder, and use a dust mask. If you need to do extensive leveling and smoothing, consider using a liquid underlayment. Consult your concrete products supplier and flooring supplier for recommendations.

Break slick surfaces. Adhesives will not bond well to a concrete floor with a slick surface. Test to see if the surface has been sealed by sprinkling water on the slab. If the water beads, you'll have to remove the sealer in order to make a bondable surface. To break the sheen caused by paint, sealers, or a steel trowel finish, sand the concrete lightly with sandpaper wrapped over a block of wood. Wear a dust mask to avoid inhaling the dust. For large or very hard surfaces, you will have to scarify (scratch) the floor with special tools or machines which are available from tool rental agencies.

Consider moisture conditions. Not all flooring materials need to be installed over a smooth surface, but *all* floor-ing needs to be laid over a dry one. The single most common problem with on-grade and below-grade concrete slabs is that they are prone to moisture collection. There are several factors which contribute to this.

Moisture problems might issue from outside the building, where downspouts are not properly directing roof water away from the foundation line. In addition, the grade or slope of the earth around the building may be both insufficient and poorly oriented, so that water tends to collect at the building's base, and from there, gets absorbed into the slab. Or perhaps there is no sub-surface drainage system around the perimeter of the building, which might cause excessive amounts of moisture to collect in the surrounding soil.

These moisture conditions are fairly easy to correct. You can reorient downspouts to carry water away from the slab, you can recut the grade to give a minimum half-inch-to-the-foot slope so that runoff water is carried well away from the slab, or you can install a subsurface drain pipe around the perimeter of the slab.

Concrete, no matter how old and well-cured, is a water-permeable material. Unless a moisture barrier was laid over the soil before a below-grade or on-grade slab was poured, the slab may wick up moisture from the ground.

Test for moisture. A simple test to determine whether moisture is wicking up through the concrete is to tape a 2-foot by 2-foot square of clear plastic to the floor and leave it for 1 or 2 days. If small droplets of water form under the plastic or if the plastic looks cloudy, there may be a moisture problem.

In addition, if a slab has alkali deposits on the exposed concrete surface; or if the finish flooring over the slab feels wet or damp, or looks puffy, buckled, or eroded from beneath the surface, this indicates a moisture problem. It should be corrected before you install a new finish floor.

Unless you have a lot of experience with concrete, moisture conditions can be tricky to assess and hard to correct. You may find it worthwhile to hire a contractor who can give you an evaluation, recommend corrective measures, and carry them out if necessary.

Moisture Test

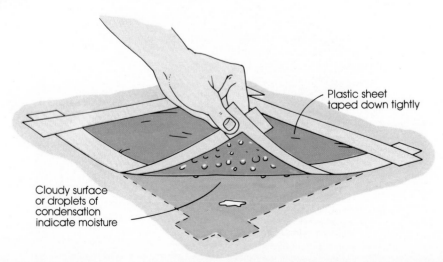

Plastic sheet taped down tightly

Cloudy surface or droplets of condensation indicate moisture

Wood Sleeper Subfloors

Wood sleeper subfloors can be installed over a concrete slab to form the subfloor structure for various types of finish materials. Usually this is done to provide a nailable surface for those types of flooring materials that cannot be fastened by other means. Wood-frame subfloors also tend to be more resilient and warmer underfoot than concrete, but not all flooring materials are appropriately installed over this type of system.

While the instructions and illustration below show 2 by 4 sleepers laid on the slab, sometimes sleeper systems are constructed with up to an 18-inch crawl or ventilation space below the subfloor surface itself. This is most often done when the concrete slab suffers from serious moisture problems or surface defects which can't otherwise be accommodated. In any case, your flooring dealer, your local building department, or a professional contractor advise you.

Constructing a wood subfloor over concrete. Sweep the concrete slab clean, seal it with asphalt primer, and spread a layer of asphalt mastic over its entire surface,

⅛ inch to ¼ inch thick. Lay 15-pound building paper or sheets of 6-mil plastic sheeting over the mastic, overlapping the edges by 6 inches. Walk over the surface to press the paper or plastic into the mastic. Snap chalklines every 16 inches across the width of the floor. Then lay short lengths of preservative-treated 2 by 4s along the chalklines. These will serve as sleepers, or support members. Leave a ½-inch to ¾-inch clearance between the ends of the sleepers and at the walls to allow for air circulation. Check the sleepers for level with a long straightedge, and shim them as needed. Nail the sleepers to the slab with concrete nails long enough to prevent them from moving. Nail either a ⅝-inch or ¾-inch plywood subfloor over the sleepers, leaving a ¹⁄₁₆-inch to ⅛-inch gap between panels, and a ½-inch gap at the walls. Provide under-floor ventilation to prevent musty odors or possible rot. Cut out 2-inch by 8-inch sections of the plywood subfloor along the two walls which are perpendicular to the direction of the sleepers. Make these cutouts at 6-foot intervals, and cover them with floor register grills after installing the finish floor.

Wood Sleeper Subfloor Construction

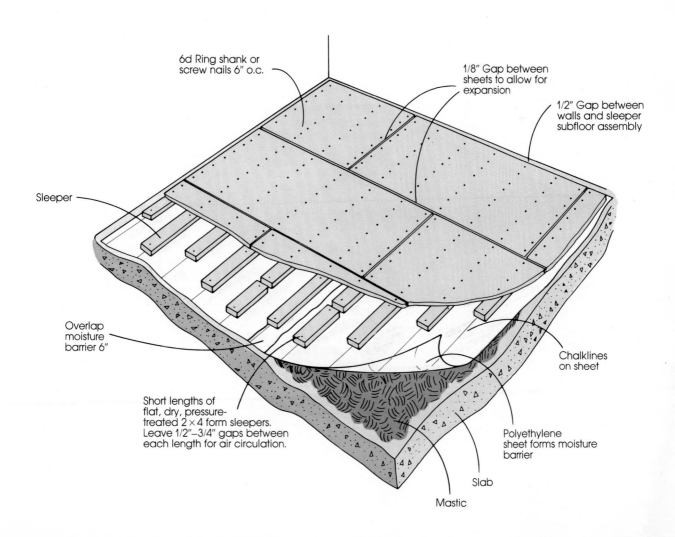

6d Ring shank or screw nails 6" o.c.

1/8" Gap between sheets to allow for expansion

1/2" Gap between walls and sleeper subfloor assembly

Sleeper

Overlap moisture barrier 6"

Short lengths of flat, dry, pressure-treated 2 × 4 form sleepers. Leave 1/2"–3/4" gaps between each length for air circulation.

Chalklines on sheet

Polyethylene sheet forms moisture barrier

Slab

Mastic

PREPARING A WOOD SUBFLOOR

Most preparation tasks for wood subfloors involve surface repairs or require the installation of a new underlayment over existing floors. The charts on pages 43, 44, 46, and 49 outline the preparation guidelines needed for installing each of the four main types of flooring. To select specific underlayment materials for your particular job, see the facing page. To remove flooring to accomplish proper preparation, see pages 52–53. To make surface repairs, see the following suggestions for correcting some common problems.

Squeaks are caused by movement between parts of the floor structure, such as the subfloor and the finish floor. The source of a squeak might be nails that have worked loose, or boards that have shrunk or cupped. Locate the squeak and re-anchor the loose flooring using 6- or 8-penny nails. Spiral or ringshank nails driven at an angle work best, since both the threads and the angle give the nails extra bite. If the squeak persists, drill pilot holes and countersink wood screws through the floor into the joists below.

Cracks, voids, and small depressions can be filled. Use a filler that is compatible with any sealers or adhesives you plan to use later. Most fillers are water-based

or latex-based, and need to be mixed just before you use them because their setup time is very fast. Clean the area of dust and debris so the filler will adhere. Trowel the filler into the crack or depression and feather its edges into the rest of the floor as smoothly as you can with a wide putty knife. Since the material dries very hard, smooth and feather it as fully as possible while it is still pliable. After it dries, sand the filled areas so that they are smooth and flush with the surrounding floor.

Warped boards and high spots can be sanded or chiseled down to produce a smooth level surface. To avoid damaging your chisel, nail the board securely first, and set the nailheads. If a board is badly warped, remove that section; drill a line of holes across each end of the defective section. Break the line with a chisel, and remove the section. Chisel the remaining rough ends smooth, and install a piece of wood to match, or build up the hole with filler.

Slick surfaces need to be roughened if you plan to use adhesives to install your new floor, since the sheen makes a poor bonding surface. A light sanding using a long-handled floor or wall sanding block is the best method.

Laying Building Paper

Some underlayment fasteners

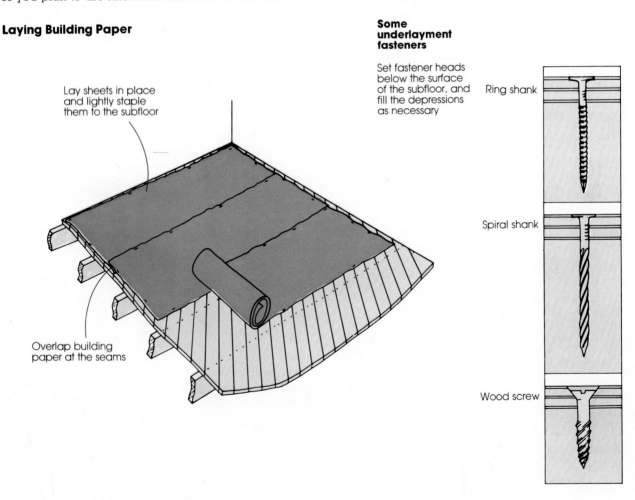

Lay sheets in place and lightly staple them to the subfloor

Overlap building paper at the seams

Set fastener heads below the surface of the subfloor, and fill the depressions as necessary

Ring shank

Spiral shank

Wood screw

About Underlayments

Underlayments can equilibrate uneven subfloor surfaces and provide an appropriately smooth surface for the finish floor. They inhibit dust, drafts, moisture, and other undesirable elements from entering the room through the floor. They can serve to join building materials that might otherwise be incompatible, and some underlayments also afford additional structural strength.

Plywood is made of an odd number of thin sheets of wood (called veneers or plies) that are glued cross-grain, and laminated together under pressure. It has a great deal of dimensional stability, and is not inclined to warp, buckle, twist, cup, or split. Because of its inherent rigidity, plywood underlayment adds structural strength, bridges gaps, and equilibrates irregularities or uneven conditions in the subfloor surface quite well. It is sold in a range of grades, thicknesses, and sheet sizes.

Underlayment grade plywood is made to satisfy the general subsurface requirements of most types of finish floors. It will hold nails and fasteners well, has no interply voids, has smooth outer faces since surface defects have been plugged and touch-sanded, and is considered water-proof.

Particle board, also known as chip board and wafer board, is made of softwood chips that have been glued together, formed and compressed into sheets under heat and pressure. The material is, therefore, very dense and smooth surfaced, free of voids or knots. But since it has no continuous grain, particle board has less inherent rigidity and structural strength though it is able to bridge minor irregularities in the subfloor. Like plywood, it is sold in various grades, thicknesses, and sheet sizes, and some particle board materials are made with water-proof glues.

Hardboard is a fine-fiber particle board made from wood pulp which has been formed into sheets. It is quite dense, somewhat brittle, difficult to nail, and adds little structural strength. It comes in a limited range of thicknesses, though it is available in several sheet sizes.

Liquid underlayments are used to smooth, even out, level, fill, patch, and even moisture-proof floor surfaces needing these types of repair. Although a few products are suitable for non-professional installation, most entail several application steps and these require a professional's skill and experience.

Installing a Wood Sheet Underlayment

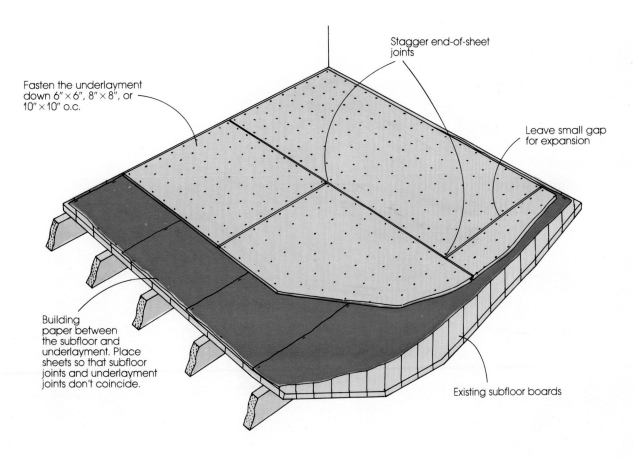

Stagger end-of-sheet joints

Fasten the underlayment down 6″ × 6″, 8″ × 8″, or 10″ × 10″ o.c.

Leave small gap for expansion

Building paper between the subfloor and underlayment. Place sheets so that subfloor joints and underlayment joints don't coincide.

Existing subfloor boards

CHAPTER 3

INSTALLATION

In this chapter you'll learn how to install
nine different types of floors, and how to
trim them out. It includes a special section
describing techniques for refinishing
existing wood floors, or finishing new ones.

Although the right choice of materials and proper preparation of the subsurface are critical to producing a successful floor, the installation techniques themselves make the final difference in any flooring project. This chapter provides you with step-by-step guidelines for installing each type of flooring yourself, and the information you need to make appropriate decisions if you'll be working with a professional.

The first two pages focus on the beginning step of a quality installation: layout. The final look of the new floor will be affected by the alignment of patterns, grout lines, wood grain, carpet pile, or other repetitive features of the material; careful layout will ensure tight joints and well-matched seams. By using a precise layout to guide the installation, you ensure that the last piece of material installed will be as accurately placed as the first. Layout can also compensate for the fact that a room's corners may not be square, or walls may not be straight; the flooring itself can visually mask these defects rather than exaggerate them.

The balance of the chapter illustrates installation techniques. These require varying degrees of skill, strength, and experience. All the installations described in this chapter are within the abilities of most do-it-yourselfers, though some are more technically exacting than others. The main requirements are the proper tools and the ability to apply these techniques to your particular situation. In many cases, you may want to use a helper.

◀

Dark wood floors sparkle by day under a flood of sunshine, and gleam by night against contrasting white walls and furnishings. Wood floors can be dressed up or down, and graciously wear the effects of age with a pleasing patina.

In terms of time, flooring for an average-sized room can be installed in less than a day with resilient material, carpet, or prefinished wood. Unfinished wood will take an additional 2 to 3 days for sanding and finishing, and ceramic tile floors will take the same amount of time for grouting—and longer if they must be sealed as well. The drying time of adhesives and grouts will affect the overall installation time.

The first section on installation describes techniques for various types of wood floors—tongue-and-groove strip, square-edge strip, tongue-and-groove plank, and parquet. This section includes step-by-step instructions for blind-nailing square-edge flooring, countersinking and plugging screwholes, and creating borders, as well as a special section on refinishing techniques for wood floors.

The next section features resilient materials. You will learn the techniques for a beautiful and lasting installation of resilient sheet goods, as well as tiles, a popular do-it-yourself material.

If you have selected ceramic tile for your floor, such as glazed or quarry tile, the next section will show you the techniques for installing it properly. You will learn how to align and set tiles with neat, uniform grout spaces, and how to grout and seal the floor.

The last section covers the installation of both conventional and cushion-backed carpet. Even if you prefer to have a professional install conventional carpet, you may want to put down the tackless strip or install the pad yourself.

Whichever materials you use, installation is really complete only when the trim is replaced or installed and the doors rehung. The last two pages of the book guide this phase of installation. Then finally, you can move your furniture back in and enjoy your new floor.

BASIC LAYOUT TECHNIQUES

Layout is a critical process that determines both how the finished floor will look and how smoothly your work will proceed. Use the guidelines below to determine to what degree the room is in square. Then, decide on which type of layout is most appropriate. Some special layout considerations, unique to each type of flooring material, are discussed in detail in Chapter 1.

Tests and Techniques for Layout

In construction terminology, rooms or walls are "in square" if the walls meet at right angles (90 degrees), or are precisely perpendicular to each other. Walls that are "out of square" create an irregularly shaped floor. Small irregularities can be overlooked, but walls that are badly out of square can clash with lines in the flooring material. The issue, then, becomes choosing the wall or walls to which you orient or "square" the floor layout.

Before starting the installation, identify the cuts or adjustments in the material you'll have to make. Rigid flooring materials won't conform to a wall that bows outward or wanders inward; if baseboards and shoe moldings won't conceal the irregularity, you'll have to cut the material to conform to it.

Regardless of which layout method you use, when you come to specific installations, you'll need to test whether a line or wall is in square to some other line or wall. A carpenter's square works for testing very small dimensions, but for the larger dimensions common in flooring installations, you need to use a classic carpenter's method called the 3-4-5 triangle.

Is the room in square? To determine if the room is in square, measure both of its diagonals—that is, the distance between opposite corners as measured through the center of the room. If the two measurements are equal, the room is square and you're safe to orient the flooring parallel to or perpendicular to any of the walls.

If not, the next step is to find which corners, if any, are in square. For a quick check, lay a carpenter's square on the floor at each corner. If it fits any of the corners perfectly, measure them again with a 3-4-5 triangle (see below) to double-check.

If two adjacent corners are in square, then only one of the four walls is out of square. If it is an obscure wall, square the layout to the remaining three walls. If it is a dominant wall, a focal point in the room, or a very long uninterrupted wall, square the layout to it or to an "average" of its orientation and that of the opposite wall.

Are the walls straight? A quick way to check a wall to see if it's straight is to measure out a distance of ¾ inch from both corners. Snap a chalkline between those points. You will immediately see any deviations between the straight chalkline and the wall.

3-4-5 triangle. This test determines whether two intersecting lines are exactly perpendicular. Start at their intersection and measure out 3 feet along one line and 4 feet along the other, marking those positions. Now measure between the two marks. If this distance is exactly 5 feet, the intersecting lines are perpendicular to each other. For larger rooms, use multiples of 3, 4, and 5 feet, such as 6, 8, and 10 foot measurements.

Checking the Room

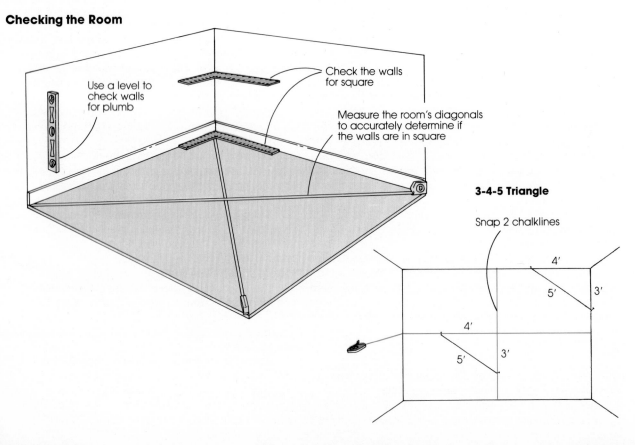

Use a level to check walls for plumb

Check the walls for square

Measure the room's diagonals to accurately determine if the walls are in square

3-4-5 Triangle

Snap 2 chalklines

4'
5'
3'
4'
5'
3'

Methods for Layout

There are three methods of layout, and the best one to use depends on three factors: the aesthetic effect you want to create, the unique characteristics of the flooring material, and the condition of existing walls.

Perimeter method. This method consists of establishing lines around the four edges of the floor, either to establish the inside edges of a border so that they are in square with the flooring field, or to keep a ceramic tile installation aligned in both directions.

Since the four walls of the room may be out of square, it is important, in laying out the lines, to keep them perfectly squared to each other rather than to the walls. The lines' distance from the wall should match the full width of the border, plus any allowances you'll have to make for expansion space, for grout lines, or for irregularities in the wall.

Starter-line method. This method of layout is for installations that begin with a single course, or line of flooring, established along one wall. It is used for wood strip and plank installations that do not have a border. It is an easy method to use, since you start laying the flooring at one end of the room with the first course aligned exactly with the starter line, and work across to the opposite wall.

Your choice of the starting wall depends on the direction in which you'll install the flooring, and other aesthetic concerns. Since the starting wall may be out of square with the room as a whole, establish the starting line by measuring back to it from the room's imaginary centerline rather than taking measurements from the wall itself. Because the wall and the starter line won't necessarily be parallel, the expansion gap may be tapered. This can be covered by baseboard; if the baseboard won't fully conceal the gap, a tapered piece of strip flooring will need to be cut to fit. If your installation includes a border, use the perimeter method to establish your borders, and then use the starter-line method to lay out and install the field—the main portion of the floor.

Quadrant method. This method consists of dividing the room into four equal sections, or quadrants, in order to start the installation in the center of the room. It is used for tile floors (wood block, resilient, and sometimes ceramic) in which the center portion of the room is the visually dominant area—the one you want your eye to fall on when you enter or use the room. In addition, if a room has walls that are out of square, or if there are jogs and nooks, cabinetry, or other elements that project from the wall, this method gives you an accurate starting point. It is also the method to use when you want to lay the tile diagonally, relative to the room as a whole. Essentially, the quadrant method allows you to create a symmetrical layout in the room and to finish the installation at opposite walls with cut tiles of equal size.

Establish the centerpoint by measuring the midpoints of both facing sets of walls, and snapping two chalklines between them, exactly perpendicular to each other. Begin the installation of each quadrant at the intersecting perpendicular lines, and proceed out along each axis.

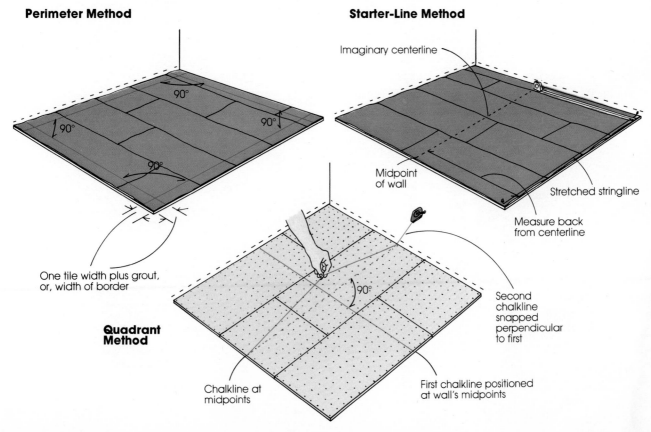

Perimeter Method

90°   90°   90°

One tile width plus grout, or, width of border

Starter-Line Method

Imaginary centerline

Midpoint of wall

Stretched stringline

Measure back from centerline

Quadrant Method

90°

Second chalkline snapped perpendicular to first

Chalkline at midpoints

First chalkline positioned at wall's midpoints

TONGUE-AND-GROOVE STRIP

Generally, strip flooring is installed perpendicular to the floor joists. If you're installing a new wood floor over existing strip flooring, however, it will run perpendicular to the existing flooring's direction. If the room would look better with the strips running parallel to the joists, the subflooring must be at least ¾ inch thick and very sound.

You can determine the direction and position of the joists by looking at the subfloor's nailing pattern. Because you will need to know the exact locations of the joists later on, indicate the center of each joist along the walls. Do not mark this on the floor, because it will be covered by building paper.

Prepare door openings. To avoid cutting and fitting the flooring material around complicated door trim, saw off the bottoms of all door casings and door stops (but not door jambs). Guide the saw with a scrap piece of flooring so that the saw's blade cuts the trim exactly high enough for the flooring material to slide under it snugly. Prepare the subfloor, mark and remove doors if necessary, and remove baseboards (see page 51).

Install 15-pound felt building paper. Cover the floor with 15-pound asphalt-saturated felt building paper laid perpendicular to the direction of the new flooring.

Overlap all edges 4 inches, and neatly trim the wall ends of the paper so the paper lies flat. Staple or tack it in place.

Snap chalklines. Referring to the joist position marks on the wall, snap a chalkline onto the building paper, over the center of each joist, to guide nailing.

Next, select the wall you will use as your starting point. To make sure the first course of flooring (row of boards) is properly aligned, you need a perfectly straight line as a guide. To make this line, measure out ¾ inch at each end of the starting wall, and mark those positions on the floor. Fasten a nail at each mark, and stretch a string line between them. (The ¾-inch space, which allows expansion of the flooring, will later be covered by baseboard or shoe molding.)

Note: If the starting wall is not square with the rest of the room (check by measuring the room's diagonals) find the midpoints of the two adjacent walls. Then make sure the starting wall stringline is the same distance from both midpoints. If it isn't, reposition the nails to hold the stringline so that it is. This technique will assure that the room looks in square, because the flooring will register to the centerline of the room.

Laying Building Paper

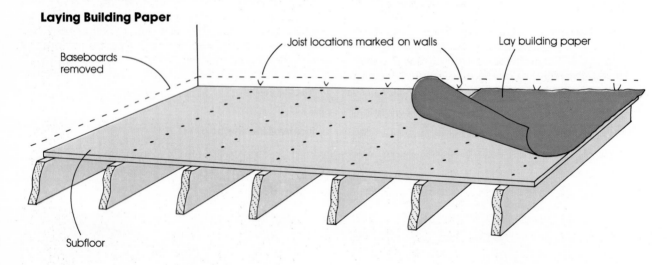

Baseboards removed

Joist locations marked on walls

Lay building paper

Subfloor

Snapping Chalklines

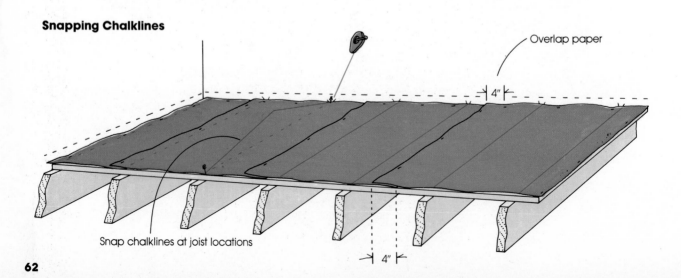

Overlap paper

4"

Snap chalklines at joist locations

4"

Install the starter course. For the first row of boards (the starter course), select a long straight flooring board and lay it against the starter line at the left side of the room so that the board's end is ½ inch from the adjacent side wall. (The left side is the side to your left when you are standing with your back to the starting wall.) Lay the board so that the tongue edge faces into the room, and the back edge is ¾ inch from the starting wall. Carefully align the groove edge along the starter line and then, beginning from the left, face-nail the board with 8-penny finish nails into the joists and every 8 to 12 inches between them. Since face-nailing can split the board quite easily, it is best to predrill for each nail.

Next, blind-nail the tongue edge by hand. Drive nails at a 45-degree angle at every joist and at the midpoints between them. Set their heads below the surface with a nailset, being careful not to mar the face or tongue of the board. Complete the starter course with additional boards. Cut the last board ½ inch short of the side wall, and use the cutoff piece to start the next course.

Hand-nail the next two courses. To ensure a random joint pattern in the finished floor, loosely arrange the next seven or eight courses of boards, mixing long and short lengths. (This process is called racking the floor.) Be sure all joints stagger at least 6 inches. Begin each course with the cutoff piece from the end of the previous course. Then nail the second and third courses from left to right. Blind-nail through the tongue at each joist, at the midpoints between joists, and 2 inches from each board end. Be sure every board has at least two nails in it, no matter how short it is.

Machine-nail the field courses. The rest of the flooring, except for the last three courses, can be installed with a

Starter Course

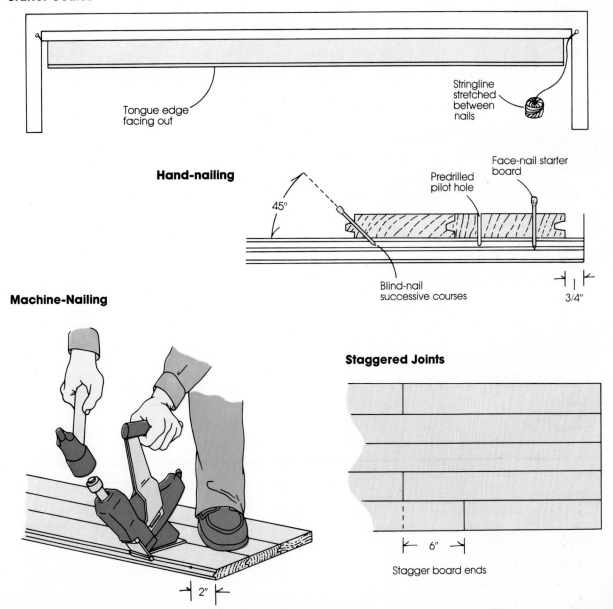

Tongue edge facing out

Stringline stretched between nails

Hand-nailing

45°

Predrilled pilot hole

Face-nail starter board

Blind-nail successive courses

3/4"

Machine-Nailing

2"

Staggered Joints

6"

Stagger board ends

TONGUE-AND-GROOVE STRIP
CONTINUED

nailing machine. Start nailing each board 2 inches from its left end. Stand on the previously nailed courses so that your toes can hold down the board being nailed. Place the shoe flange of the nailing machine on the board's edge and hit the plunger with the rubber mallet, using a firm but easy swing of the mallet. Continue nailing in the same pattern used for the first three courses, always moving from left to right along each course. If the flooring gets out of square for several courses, nail tighter on one end of the course, and looser on the other, until the problem is corrected. Make the adjustment over enough courses so you don't end up with gaps.

Special situations. If there is a hallway or closet along the starting wall, you'll need to reverse the direction of the tongue edge. To do this, glue a slip-tongue or spline into the groove of the starter strip and proceed to install the reversed flooring courses.

If the floor has register holes, posts, or other obstructions, cut and fit the flooring around them as you come to each one. In some cases you may want to frame a decorative border around the obstruction. Use a miter box to cut 45-degree angles on the board ends, and remove the exposed tongue by ripping the board on a table saw.

Reversing the Direction

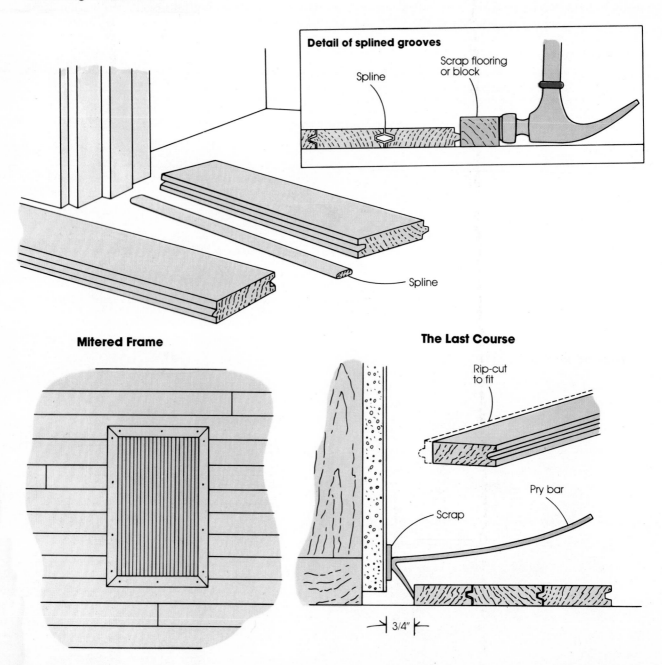

Detail of splined grooves

Spline

Scrap flooring or block

Spline

Mitered Frame

The Last Course

Rip-cut to fit

Pry bar

Scrap

3/4"

Install the last three courses. As you approach the opposite wall, there will not be enough room to use the nailing machine. Blind-nail the third course from the last by hand; the last two courses must be face-nailed. As you face-nail these courses, snug each board into position with a prybar. Install the last course leaving a ¾-inch gap along the wall. You may have to ripcut boards or cut off their tongues to fill the remaining space.

Install a threshold. Where the strip flooring meets other flooring materials, usually in door openings, you need to provide a smooth and safe transition. Use a tapered threshold, stained and finished to match the strip flooring, or, where surface heights are the same, cover the joint with a flat metal bar.

Fill cracks and nail holes in all face-nailed boards. Use a floor filler for unfinished floors or a color-matched putty stick for prefinished floors. Next, sand, stain, and finish unfinished floors as desired (see pages 70–73 for finishing techniques). Prefinished floors will probably need a light cleaning and buffing to remove dirt and scuffs caused by the installation process.

Finish the floor and replace the base molding. Nail the baseboard back into the wall studs. If there is a shoe molding as well, nail it to the baseboard and not to the strip flooring, so that the flooring can expand and contract freely underneath it. See page 92.

Installing the Threshold

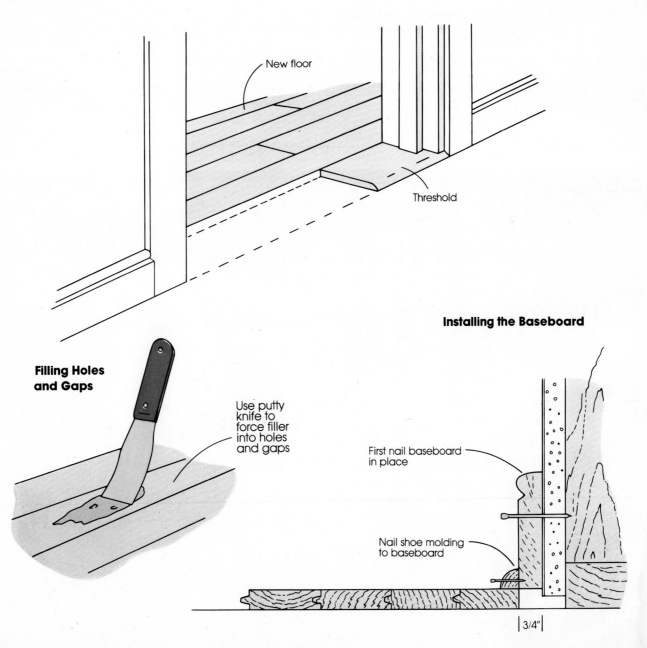

New floor

Threshold

Filling Holes and Gaps

Use putty knife to force filler into holes and gaps

Installing the Baseboard

First nail baseboard in place

Nail shoe molding to baseboard

3/4"

SQUARE-EDGE STRIP

Square-edge flooring is less costly than tongue-and-groove because of its reduced thickness ($\frac{5}{16}$ inch, $\frac{3}{8}$ inch and $\frac{1}{2}$ inch) and lesser milling waste. However, it requires face-nailing and nail-holes must be filled. Square-edge strip is usually 2 inches wide. Plank is available in various widths, sometimes with beveled edges or V-joints.

Stretch stringlines. Stretch the starter stringline as described on page 61. If you want to place a border all around the room (usually five or six boards deep), stretch stringlines along the two side walls and back wall, squaring all of them to the starter line (see the perimeter method of layout, page 61.)

Install the starter course. Lay a long strip of flooring inside the starter stringline, leaving a $\frac{3}{4}$-inch gap at the walls. Baseboard and shoe molding will cover this gap. Predrill nail holes at the board's ends, to prevent splitting. Keeping the board's edge aligned with the stringline, face-nail the board with two 1-inch flooring nails every 7 inches. Finish the starter course.

Floor with a border. If you are installing a border, install the end wall course next, and then the side wall courses to butt tightly between the starter and end wall courses. See the illustrations below.

Install the second course, beginning with the starting wall and left end wall. Use a miter box to cut a square end on the piece that ends each course. Snug each piece firmly against the first course by driving a screwdriver or chisel against its edge into the subfloor, and use your knee to gain leverage. Use only enough nails to hold the board in place, but always nail in line with the 7-inch nailing pattern. Stagger the joints between boards. As you complete each concentric border, begin the next one at the starter wall, proceed to the end wall, and finish with the side walls.

Floor without a border. Working from the starter course, loosely lay out courses of boards so that you can check the appearance of the joint patterns before nailing. When satisfied, snug the first piece against the starter course with the aid of a screwdriver or chisel as described above. Continue nailing boards in place. When you reach the final course you may have to rip or taper the boards to fit. Go back over the floor and finish nailing. A rented pneumatic nailer will speed the process.

To keep the nailing lines straight, snap chalklines or hold a long straightedge against the row you are nailing. Set the nail heads, and fill the holes and cracks with wood filler. Sand the floor with coarse-, then medium-, and then fine-grit sandpaper. Stain and finish as desired. Reinstall trim.

Establishing the Layout

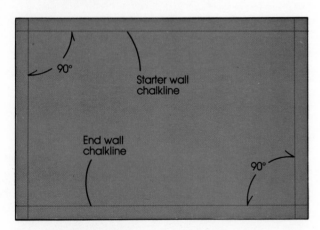

Installing the Border

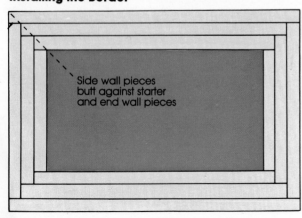

Side wall pieces butt against starter and end wall pieces

Starter Course Detail

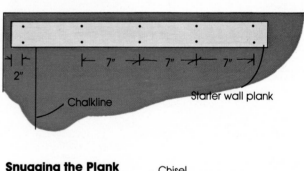

Snugging the Plank

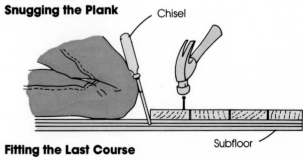

Fitting the Last Course

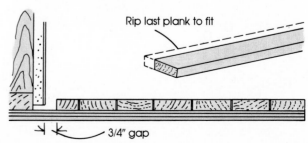

INSTALLING
TONGUE-AND-GROOVE PLANK

Install the planks. Tongue-and-groove planks are installed the same way as tongue-and-groove strips, by face-nailing the starter boards and blind-nailing the field courses. With plank floors, however, the material may come in random widths, and you'll need to pay close attention to the pattern they will make. Inventory the stock before installation to see how many boards (or how much total length) you have for each width. Then plan your installation so that the boards make an attractive pattern and so you'll be able to finish the floor with the same pattern you start with. You don't want to use up a particular width of board too soon.

Install the plugs. Some manufactured products include wooden plugs at the ends of each board to simulate the pegged floors of bygone days. Install this flooring as you would other plank flooring, but first decide what plug pattern you want to establish. Keep these points in mind. Since you must cut boards to fit each time you end a course, these boards will have no plug holes at one end. If you use the cut-off piece to start a new course, it too, will have no plug holes at one end. You can counterbore the screw holes and plug them to maintain the pattern of plugs. If you use a new board to begin each

course, you'll have a continuous row of plugs along the left wall which you'll want to duplicate along the right wall so that the edges match. To reduce the number of plugs across the floor's edge, you can cut one end off the beginning board and use the cut-off piece at the end of the course. Where you reduce the screw positions, plan to blind-nail the plank securely to the subfloor surface below.

Measure and mark the position for the plugs at the end of each board. A 3½-inch board usually gets one plug, a 6-inch board two, and an 8-inch board three. For wide planking, pay particular attention to the nailing schedule (see page 42), as wider planks need the additional fastening. Drill pilot holes at all the marks for screws, and counterbore them for the size plug you are using. (If you want the plugs to be made of another wood not available at your supplier, you can cut your own with a plug-cutting bit.) Screw down the flooring using No. 9 wood screws. Then glue and tap a plug into each hole. Chisel each plug off to nearly flush with the floor surface; they will be brought fully flush when the floor is sanded for finishing. Install thresholds, baseboards, and other trim, and sand and finish the floor.

Tongue-and-Groove Plank Floors

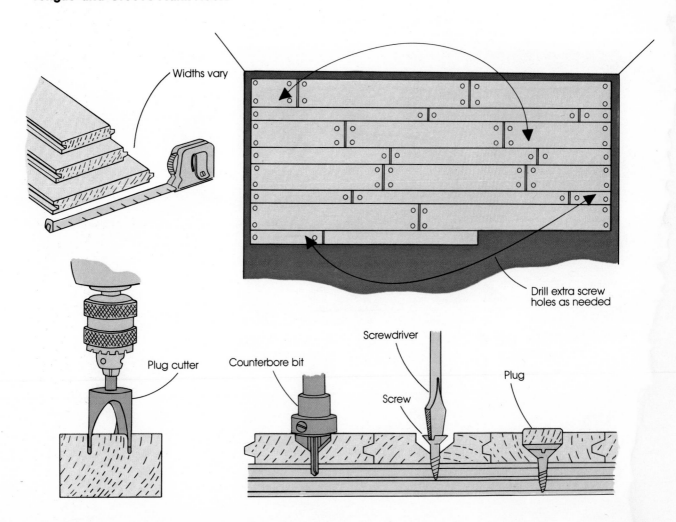

Widths vary

Drill extra screw holes as needed

Plug cutter

Counterbore bit

Screwdriver

Screw

Plug

WOOD BLOCK & PARQUET

Wood block and parquet flooring are tile materials. To install them, you'll use the quadrant method of layout (see page 61). Find the midpoints of the two side walls and snap a line between them. Snap a second chalkline perpendicular to the first, using the midpoint of the end walls to position it. Before snapping the line, however, square it to the first chalkline by measuring a 3-4-5 triangle (see page 60). These are preliminary layout lines, which may have to be moved toward or away from a wall after the test run (see below), although the lines must still be kept perfectly square to each other.

If your pattern is to be laid on a diagonal, repeat the process by snapping a second set of chalklines at a 45-degree offset from the first (see page 77). Be sure the diagonal lines are square to each other. Make a test run and adjust guidelines until you have a layout that pleases you.

Try out the layout with a test run. Begin the test layout with one of the quadrants that leads to the room's entrance. Start at the chalkline intersection and work toward both walls. At the room's entrance, you want a row

of full-size blocks. Therefore, when your test run reaches the entrance wall, adjust it so full blocks will end there, allowing for a ½-inch gap along the wall. If the room has another entrance on an adjacent wall, repeat the process on an axis leading to that wall. This sets a new intersection so that any cut tiles will fall on side or back walls. With the test run completed, adjust the chalklines accordingly. *Note:* In most cases it is desirable to have full blocks at the entrance. But if they create a row of cut blocks along the opposite wall that would be more distracting than cut blocks at the entrance, adjust your layout accordingly.

Begin the first quadrant. Carefully sweep and vacuum the subfloor. Apply enough adhesive for six to eight blocks at a time, or according to manufacturer's instructions, holding the toothed trowel at a 35 to 45 degree angle. If possible, avoid covering the chalklines, or re-snap them over the adhesive.

Start the installation at the chalkline intersection and complete one quadrant at a time. Carefully position the first block so that it is well squared to both chalk-

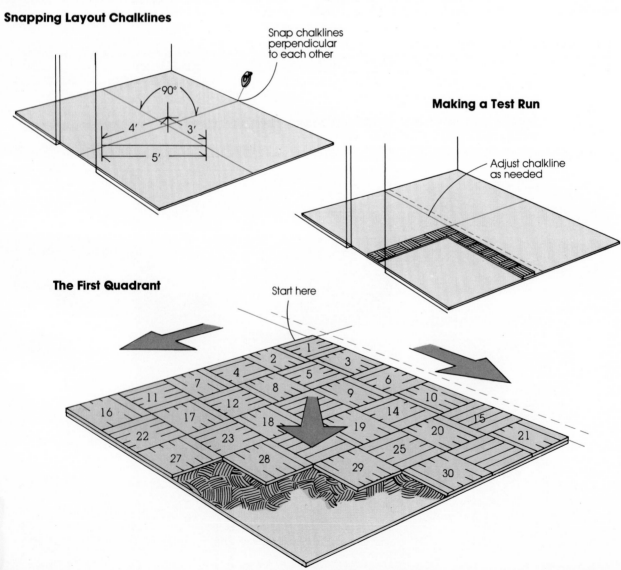

Snapping Layout Chalklines

Snap chalklines perpendicular to each other

90°

4' 3'

5'

Making a Test Run

Adjust chalkline as needed

The First Quadrant

Start here

lines. This is the "key" block for guiding the entire installation. Any errors in placement will be magnified as the installation progresses, so be careful. Lay the next few blocks along each axis, pressing each one "hand-tight" into place, and keeping all edges aligned. Fill in the area between the two axes, working your way progressively out to the walls.

Complete the first quadrant. Continue laying blocks along each axis and filling the area between. When you reach a wall, there should be a ½-inch gap between it and the last tile. This gap is for expansion of the flooring during humidity changes, and should be filled with a cork strip or other compressible material to keep the blocks from shifting.

At some point you will have to walk and kneel on newly laid blocks. Lay plywood over them to distribute your weight and to prevent displacing any blocks. Also, avoid sliding blocks into place, because this forces adhesive up into the joint, preventing a tight, clean fit. Immediately remove any adhesive that squeezes up onto the surface, using a compatible solvent. When you reach a heat register, hearth, or any other obstruction, mark and cut individual blocks to fit neatly around it. Use a fine-toothed backsaw or dovetail saw for straight cuts, and a coping saw or saber saw for curved cuts. If the cut is complex, cut an exact template from cardboard to trace onto the wood block. Then cut the block accordingly. When you need to cut blocks to fit at a wall. Use the process illustrated below for marking border tiles to fit.

Complete the remaining quadrants. Finish each quadrant as you did the first, starting at the center of the room and fanning out along both axes. When the entire floor has been installed, allow it to stand as long as the adhesive manufacturer specifies. Then install shoe molding and other trim, nailing it to the baseboard or wall and not into the flooring. Next, install door thresholds. You may need to trim doors down before hanging them (see page 50).

If the block flooring is not prefinished, sand it and apply sealing and finishing coats according to the manufacturer's instructions (see pages 70–73).

Completing the Other Quadrants

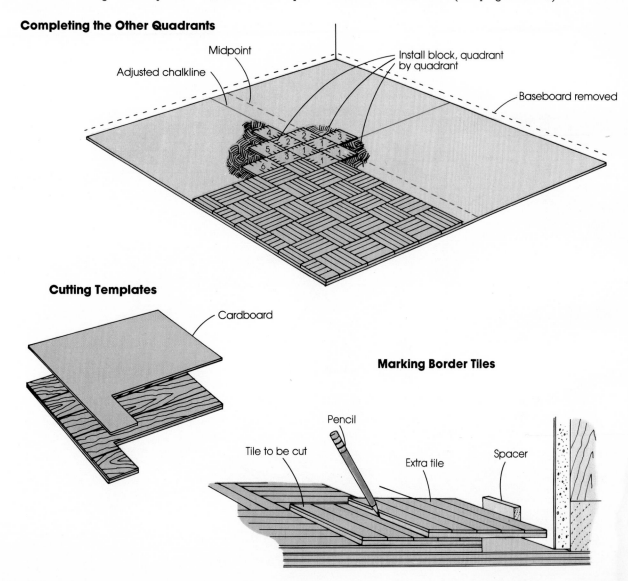

Midpoint

Adjusted chalkline

Install block, quadrant by quadrant

Baseboard removed

Cutting Templates

Cardboard

Marking Border Tiles

Pencil

Tile to be cut

Extra tile

Spacer

REFINISHING WOOD FLOORS

Before you decide to refinish your wood floor, make sure it isn't just dulled by several layers of old wax and grime that make it look like it needs refinishing. To check for this, dip fine steel wool in kerosene or alcohol, and rub in a circular motion to remove the old layers in a one-square-foot section. Wipe off the residue with a damp sponge, apply a layer of paste wax, and buff it up to a shine. If the results are satisfactory, you may have saved yourself a lot of trouble.

Clean and rewax. Before proceeding, set any protruding nails or screws and make any necessary minor repairs. Then scrub the floor with a rented buffing machine, using a steel wool or screen pad. Pour kerosene or alcohol on one small area at a time, and scrub with the machine. Mop up the residue with a damp mop (rinse often), and then allow to dry thoroughly for several hours. Apply a new coat of paste wax, then two more coats in the areas of heavier traffic, and buff with the buffing machine, using soft cotton pads.

Refinish. When your floor no longer looks nicely finished—in spite of spot repairs, stripping, and rewaxing—or when it has scratches and stains that cannot be removed, it's time to refinish. Refinishing a wood floor is a

big job, but it requires more patience and practice than special skills, and many people do it themselves with great success. Before you proceed, however, make sure the wood is thick enough to sand. To determine this, remove a floor register or pry up a piece of flooring from a closet or other inconspicuous place. If the wood is 5/16 inch thick or less, it might not take another sanding. If it's 3/4 inch thick, there is no risk of sanding through it.

Before sanding, remove all the furnishings, including curtains, and anything that's movable. Cover built-in units and doorways with plastic sheeting to contain the dust from sanding. Remove any shoe moldings and baseboards that are easily replaced; if you want to reinstall them, mark them for later identification, and remove the nails. Set any protruding floor nails 1/8 inch below the floor's surface with a nail set.

Make sure you have a dust mask ready, and shoes with clean soles (not black rubber, which may mark the wood). You may also wish to wear ear protectors, since most sanders are quite noisy.

Fill holes and gaps. The techniques and tools for refinishing wood block and parquet floors are the same for strip or plank floors. For both types, holes and gaps

Preparing and Sanding Strip Flooring

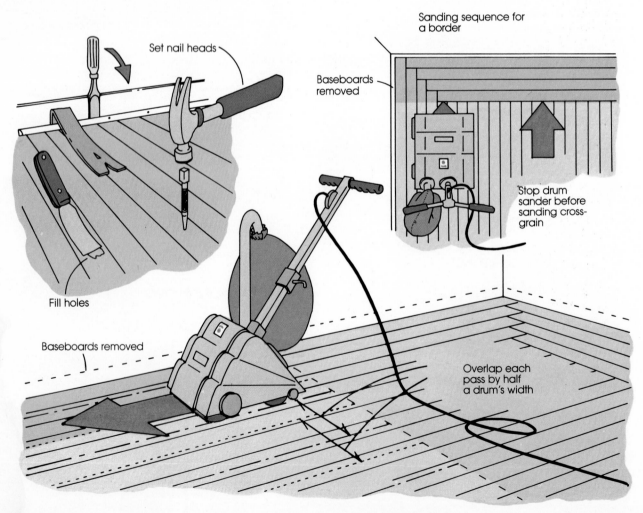

Set nail heads

Fill holes

Baseboards removed

Sanding sequence for a border

Baseboards removed

Stop drum sander before sanding cross-grain

Overlap each pass by half a drum's width

should be filled before sanding. Use a wood filler close to the same color as the bare wood—scrape a corner to get a look at the color. Apply the filler with a large putty knife. Allow the filler to dry thoroughly before beginning sanding.

Rent the equipment. Most rental agencies carry the specialized equipment required for sanding—a drum sander for the main part of the floor and a floor edger for corners and edges. Both machines are heavy-duty and require some strength to operate. Have the rental agent give you some operating instructions; not all machines are alike. Pay attention to procedures for changing sandpaper, lowering the drum, and emptying dust bags.

You will need three grades of sandpaper—coarse, medium, and fine—in both sheets and disks. Take home plenty, because you won't be charged for paper that you return unused. Six sheets and six disks of coarse-grade sandpaper, and eight each of the finer grades should be more than enough for one room. The finer grits clog up more quickly.

Start with the drum sander. The actual process of sanding with a drum sander is like flying an airplane, in that takeoffs and landings are the tricky parts. The drum itself is always rotating and should be in contact with the floor only when you are pushing or pulling the machine along the floor, and not while it is standing in one spot. You must lower the drum to the floor as you roll the machine, and raise it up just before reaching a wall or other stopping point. Otherwise, you will gouge the floor.

To begin, plug in the sander in another room, in order to keep the electrical cord out of your way. Start along the right side of the room, a few inches away from the wall and behind an imaginary centerline. Sand to-ward the wall. Then pull the sander back over the imaginary centerline and, overlapping the previous pass by half a drum-width, sand toward the wall again. When you have finished half the room this way, turn around and sand the floor on the other side of the imaginary centerline in the same manner. Always sand with the grain, unless the floor is parquet or is uneven and must be leveled.

For parquet or uneven floors, sand across the floor diagonally one way with the coarse paper, the opposite way with the medium grit, and parallel to the walls with the fine grit. Go over each section twice, first walking behind the drum sander, then pulling it back behind you. Overlap each section half the width of the drum. Use the edge sander in the same way as it is used for strip and plank floors. (See the facing page.) Finish by sanding with the grain using the finer grits.

If the floor has a border with boards laid perpendicular to the direction you are sanding, stop before sanding across their grain. When you finish the main boards, sand the border separately, going with the grain.

Sand the entire floor once with the coarse paper. It will become rough and fuzzy, so the next step is to smooth the wood by sanding it with the medium-grit paper. Check and replace your sandpaper when you don't see any action. When this second sanding is complete, fill any remaining open cracks or nail holes with a wood filler. Use a type specified for floors, and spread it with a broad putty knife. When it dries, sand the floor with the finer grits.

Sand the edges. The drum sander cannot reach every part of the floor, so you need an edger to sand along walls and in tight spaces like closets. The edger is a

Filling and Sanding Wood Block or Parquet

Fill surface as needed

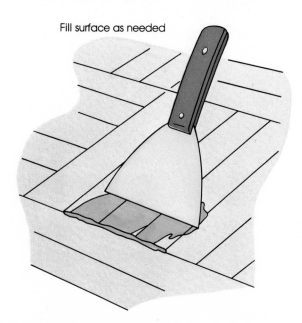

Sanding sequence and direction

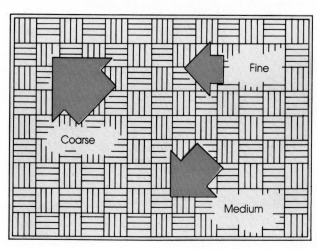

Fine

Coarse

Medium

rotary sander, and uses sandpaper disks. It is faster than the drum sander, but is also more prone to gouging, and it sands across the grain. Therefore, start out in closets or other back spaces until you get the feel of it. Using a scallop motion of small semicircles rather than a straight back-and-forth motion helps to avoid gouging. As much as possible, avoid leaning the sander to the right or left, which forces the disk to gouge across the grain. In corners where the wood strips join at right angles, turn the edger to go with the grain, and go back and forth around that turn several times. To get at corners and other spots inaccessible to the sanding machines, use a hand scraper. Finish up those spots by hand-sanding with fine paper.

Vacuum, buff, and tack the floor. Vacuum up the dust, and then check again for any holes or gaps that have been uncovered during the sanding. Fill them with putty, sand the filled areas by hand with the finest sandpaper, and then vacuum again. You may want to go over the floor with a buffing machine using fine steel wool or screen pads. This will give you a very smooth, professionally-finished-looking floor.

Next, vacuum the floor again thoroughly to remove as much dust as possible. Then remove the final residue of dust before applying the finish. To do this, use a painter's tack cloth or a terrycloth towel wrapped around a broom and moistened with alcohol or kerosene. Wipe the corners, edges, and gaps in the floor, as well as open spaces. Any dust left will be caught in the finish coats.

At this point you should also remove any stains. Apply ordinary household bleach in carefully controlled doses to stained areas. Rinse thoroughly and allow to dry. You may need to lightly sand again and vacuum the area that was bleached.

Apply the sealer or stain. It's a good idea to seal a wood floor on the same day that you give it the final sanding, so that the bare wood won't get dirty or absorb moisture from the air. Sealers can be clear, tinted in wood hues, or even colored. No matter which type you use, it is important to note that excess sealer that does not penetrate into the wood must be removed, or it will leave dark splotches that obscure the wood.

Read the manufacturer's specifications for spreading techniques. Test a spot in a back closet or on a scrap

Sanding the Edges

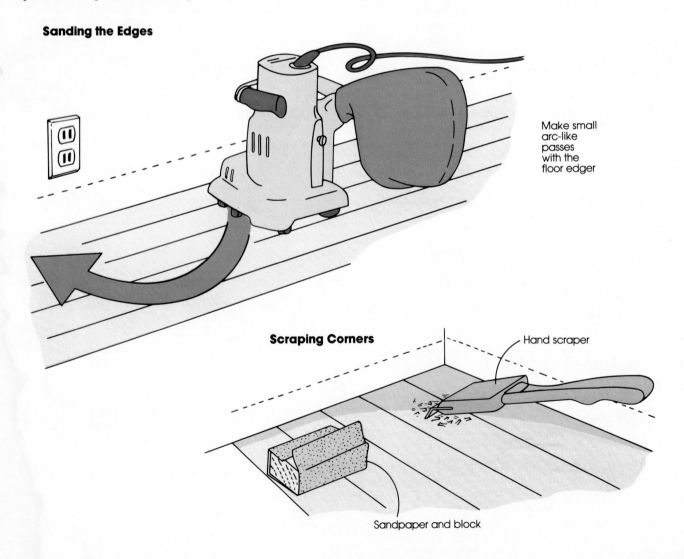

Make small arc-like passes with the floor edger

Scraping Corners

Hand scraper

Sandpaper and block

of wood to see how many coats or how much drying time gives the best results. A sheepskin applicator will spread the stain or sealer evenly without foaming it into bubbles. Or, if you use rags, wear rubber gloves. Be careful to apply sealer and stain sparingly, and wipe away any residue after 10 to 15 minutes.

Buff the floor. After the sealer dries, buff it with No. 2 fine steel wool. If the room is small, simply wrap fine steel wool around a padded 2 by 4 and buff by hand. For larger rooms, you can rent a buffer. A buffing machine requires a steady hand to operate. Start in the middle of the room to avoid banging into walls until you get used to it. You will probably need to change pads once or twice, since they clog with the excess stain or sealer. Do the corners by hand with a scrap of steel wool. After buffing, remove dust with a vacuum and tack cloth.

Apply finish. Use a finish wax or a plastic floor finish like polyurethane, and apply it according to the manufacturer's specifications. The liquid types can be applied with a paint brush or roller, although some rollers leave bubbles (a mohair roller works best). Work slowly, and brush or roll the finish with the grain. Apply two coats, with a light buffing of steel wool between them. After the second coat dries—in anywhere from 8 to 16 hours—the floor is completely finished. To be safe, wait 24 hours before moving furniture back into the room.

Floor Finishes for Wood

There are so many different sealers and finishes available that making a choice can be difficult. Go to a hardware store and look at the effects of various products on samples of the same kind of wood you have on your floor. Read the labels to determine how to apply the finish, and whether it will give you the kind of performance you want. You may want to test the effect on an inconspicuous spot, perhaps inside a closet. The different types of sealers and finishes and their characteristics are listed below, to give you a starting point in the selection process.

Penetrants

Penetrants are products that are absorbed into the wood and seal the pores of the grain against moisture and dirt; they include a variety of sealers, stains, and oils. Some penetrants can serve as final finish coats—though in most cases, the wood will still have to be covered with a more durable surface finish.

Plastic sealers. Plastic sealers such as polyurethanes are commonly used on wood floors underneath additional finish coats. They are easy to apply, and many can simply be waxed over.

Stain-sealers. These products tone or stain the wood, and semi-seal it at the same time. Some provide a matte finish and require no additional surface coats. For other types, cover with a compatible surface finish (read the label for manufacturer's instructions), and/or wax and buff. Stain-sealers are easy to apply.

Oils. Tung or linseed oils are readily absorbed by wood and provide a soft, natural finish. Some contain color stain as well. They are easy to apply and easily touched up by rubbing more oil on the floor with a soft cloth. Oil finishes do not last long, and may attract dust and dirt. Renew frequently by applying more oil. Oils are not compatible with most other finishes—once you have an oiled floor, you will have to stick with this choice. They can be waxed with a compatible paste wax once the oil is absorbed into the wood.

Stains. Stains add color or tone to wood while allowing the natural grain pattern to show through. They are not finish coats, and the floor must still be sealed, oiled, waxed, or otherwise finished with compatible products. Consult the manufacturer's label for instructions.

Surface Finishes

Shellac, varnish, lacquer, and polyurethane and other plastic finishes provide a hard, protective surface over color stains and sealers. These are intended to be permanent surface finishes. Not all share the same working characteristics, though each has certain qualities to recommend it, in terms of durability, renewability, and the particular finished look it gives.

Shellac. Shellac finishes are durable, though they do show scratches. Shellac goes on easily, spreads evenly, and dries quickly. It seals the wood's pores, and can be touched up. However, it has little resistance to water, heat, or alcohol, and it has a short container life.

Varnish. Varnish dries hard, withstands moisture, and can be rubbed or buffed to a high gloss. However, it is easily damaged by heat; and should be applied when the room is warm (about 70°). Except for fast-dry varieties, it dries slowly. Thin the first coat to be applied to bare wood by 25 percent, then use it full strength for subsequent coats. Sand between coats.

Lacquer. Lacquer is a quick-drying, heatproof, water-resistant finish which can be rubbed to a matte or glossy lustre. It can be sprayed on or applied by brush, to give a very beautiful, finished look.

Polyurethane. Polyurethane is a hard, clear, durable plastic finish which is impervious to water, alcohol, chemicals, and heat. Under normal to heavy traffic and wear, it will stay intact without chipping or cracking. It is fairly easy to apply but dries slowly, especially if humidity is high.

RESILIENT SHEET FLOORING

Before installing resilient sheet materials, there are a few room preparation steps you'll want to take. In addition to preparing the existing floor surface (see pages 44–45), remove all shoe molding or baseboards and mark pieces for later identification if you plan to reuse them. Undercut door casings just enough so the sheet flooring can slip under them.

Make rough cuts. Measure the room's dimensions accurately and mark them on a rough sketch. Include any permanent features, such as cabinets or a hearth. To make the rough cuts, roll the material out, face up, on a clean flat surface, such as a well-swept driveway or garage floor. Do not assume that the factory edges are straight or square to any pattern the flooring might have. Check them with a straightedge or snap a chalk-line to measure from. On glossy surfaces you may need to use a water-soluble felt pen. Recut the edges to square them if necessary.

Starting from the longest edge of the longest wall, begin marking out the measurements. (Add a 3-inch allowance to all edges; this excess allows adjustment of the flooring before the final trimming.) Double-check all measurements. Rough-cut the piece to size using a utility knife, shears, or rotary power cutter.

Lay the flooring in place. Roll up the flooring, face inside, so that the longest edge of the longest wall remains free. Carry it into the room and position that edge so that its 3-inch margin curls up the wall. Unroll the sheet, tugging and adjusting it so that it is essentially centered and the pattern lines are square to the room. Make relief cuts at outside and inside corners of the 3-inch margin as you proceed. Do this very carefully, slitting the corners just enough so that the margin opens to allow the flooring to lay flat. Be careful not to cut beyond the margins. To fit around a pipe or post, cut a slit from the edge of the flooring closest to the obstruction. Fit the flooring around it by making small relief cuts. When it fits, trim the flooring exactly.

Trim the edges to fit. You may need to trim twice, first to remove most of the margin, and secondly, to perfect the fit. Begin by making freehand cuts with a utility knife; feel along the edge of the floor with the knife blade, or

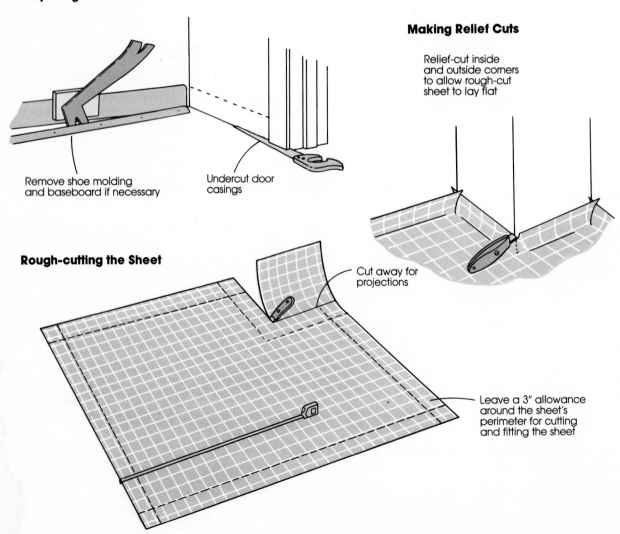

Preparing to Install

Remove shoe molding and baseboard if necessary

Undercut door casings

Making Relief Cuts

Relief-cut inside and outside corners to allow rough-cut sheet to lay flat

Rough-cutting the Sheet

Cut away for projections

Leave a 3" allowance around the sheet's perimeter for cutting and fitting the sheet use a straightedge pushed tightly against the margin's fold. Cut as you go, leaving a ⅛-inch gap along the wall to allow for expansion. The gap will later be covered by baseboard or cove molding.

Proceed carefully around the room, making sure the sheet doesn't shift position. At doorways without a threshold, trim the flooring at the centerline of the closed door. The exposed edge of the sheet will later be covered with a flat metal bar.

Glue down the flooring. Some sheets can be attached to the subfloor with a band of adhesive around the perimeter and under seams, or even installed with staples set so close to the edges that the base trim will hide them. Other sheet materials should be completely glued down with adhesive.

To apply adhesive, carefully lift up and fold half of the sheet onto the other half. Apply the adhesive to the floor with a toothed trowel according to the manufacturer's directions. Work from the corners to the center of each length of wall. Special applicators are available for hard-to-reach spots. Then unfold the sheet into place;

walk on it to press it into the adhesive. Repeat the process for the other half of the room.

Finally, use a mallet and padded block to press the flooring into the adhesive around the edges, or, if adhesive was spread over the entire floor, use a floor roller to bond the new flooring fully. You can rent a floor roller from a tool rental outlet, or from the flooring dealer. Start at the center and roll toward the edges.

Install the trim. Nail baseboard or shoe molding back in place, or install vinyl cove molding according to the manufacturer's specifications. (See page 92). Cut each length of coving to fit, only as you need to; many will be installed full-length. Bend it at the inside corners by scoring the back and cutting a V-notch at its base to create a miter joint. For outside corners, score a wide groove in the back of the cove material and bend it around the corner, but do not cut its base. Trowel adhesive onto the wall or the back of the cove material and press it into place. Use a board to force it tightly against the wall. Work your way around the room piece by piece until all the coving is installed.

Trimming Away the Allowance

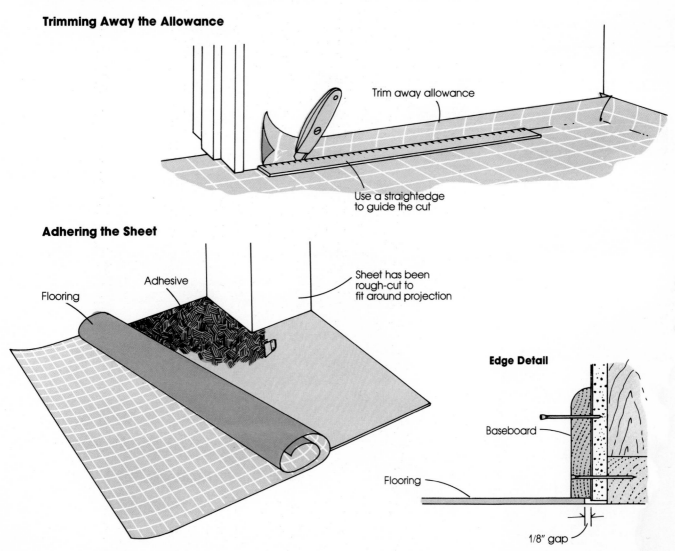

Trim away allowance

Use a straightedge to guide the cut

Adhering the Sheet

Flooring

Adhesive

Sheet has been rough-cut to fit around projection

Edge Detail

Baseboard

Flooring

1/8" gap

SEAMING RESILIENT SHEET

Install both sheets. If it is necessary to seam two sheets of resilient flooring together, use the following procedures after establishing a location that will not be too visible and that is not across a heavily trafficked area. Cut out, fit, and trim the first sheet, but leave a 3-inch margin along the edge to be seamed. Then glue (or staple) this sheet in place, stopping 8 or 9 inches short of the actual location of the seam.

Next, cut and fit the second piece; let it overlap the first sheet's seam edge by 3 inches. (If the flooring has a design or pattern, be sure to align the second sheet so that the pattern matches the first piece perfectly.) Then apply adhesive to within 5 or 6 inches of the first sheet's edge and press the second sheet into place, leaving its unglued edge overlapping the first sheet.

Cut and glue down the seam. To cut the seam, use a chalkline or a straight line in the flooring pattern for a guide, and run a sharp utility knife against a steel straightedge, cutting through both layers of flooring.

Remove the scrap pieces and glue down the seam by pulling back both edges of flooring and spreading a band of adhesive along the floor. Then join the two edges together and press the seam into the adhesive. Immediately wipe off any adhesive that oozes up, and clean the seam with a compatible solvent.

Seal the seam. After the adhesive's specified setup time, seal the seam with a special solvent that melts the seam edges enough for them to fuse together. The solvent comes in a bottle that includes a special applicator spout. Run the spout along the seam, according to directions, so that the sealer is applied only to the seam, not to the flooring. The seam should now be waterproof.

Positioning Both Pieces

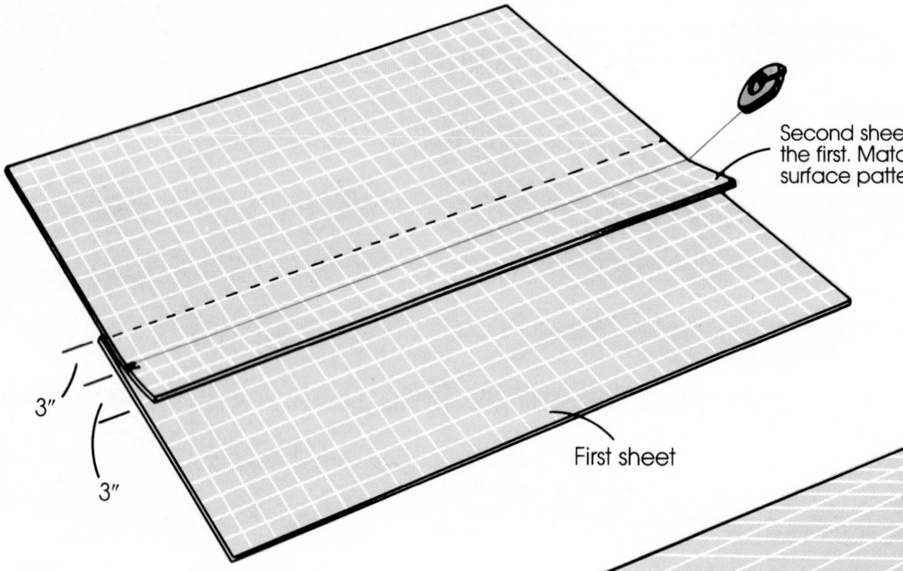

Second sheet overlaps the first. Match any surface pattern carefully.

First sheet

3"

3"

Cutting the Seam

Straightedge

Adhering Each Piece

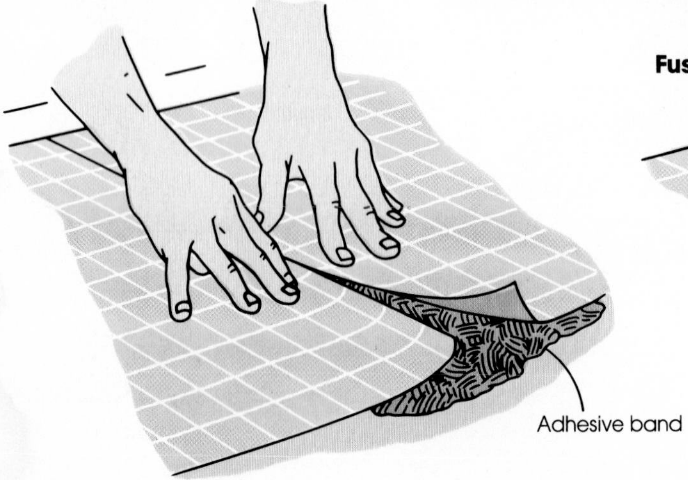

Adhesive band

Fusing the Seam

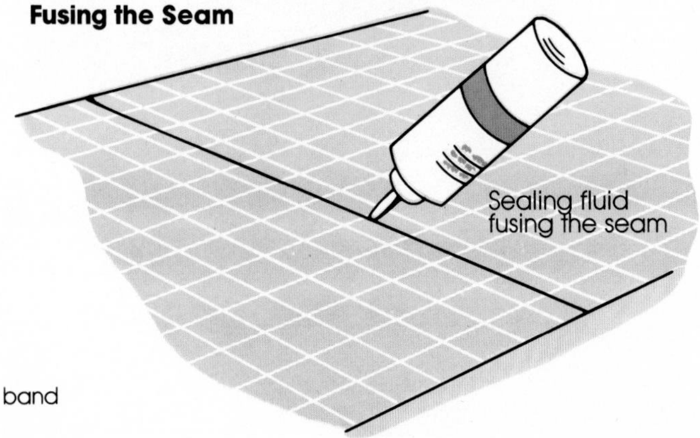

Sealing fluid fusing the seam

RESILIENT TILE FLOORS

Before beginning the installation, remove baseboards and sweep the subfloor clean. If the room has an irregular shape or several protruding obstacles, you'll find it easiest to install the tile if you use the largest rectangular portion of the room to lay out the guidelines.

Lay out and snap the chalkline. Measure and mark the midpoints of the two opposite side walls and snap a line between them. Then do the same for the two end walls; but before snapping the second chalkline, be sure it is squared to the first. To check for square, use the 3-4-5 triangle (see page 60) and adjust the chalkline accordingly.

If you are laying out a diagonal pattern, first establish guidelines, as illustrated below. Then measure 5 feet out from the lines' intersection along each axis and make a mark. Find the midpoints between these marks,

and snap a chalkline through two opposite midpoints so that the line also intersects the center. It should extend in both directions to the walls. This line should be at a 45-degree angle to the original quadrant lines. Now stretch the chalkline across the remaining two midpoints, and make sure it is perfectly squared to the first diagonal. Make adjustments as needed.

Try out the layout with a test run. Lay dry tiles along both axes of one quadrant, starting at the center and working toward the walls. If the space between the last tile and the wall is less than half a tile's width, adjust the centerline to provide enough room for at least a tile of half-width against the wall. Continue testing layouts with dry runs until the borders have a satisfying look. For the sake of durability and appearance, borders that front an opening or door areas should have full tiles.

Snapping Chalklines

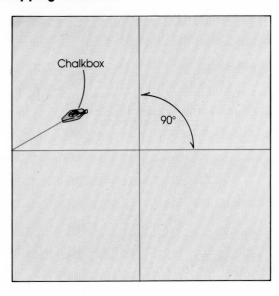

Layout for a Diagonal Installation

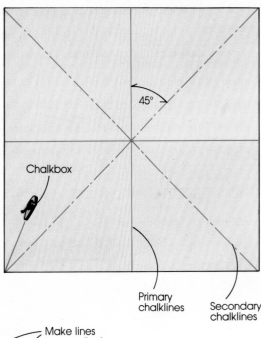

Making a Test Run

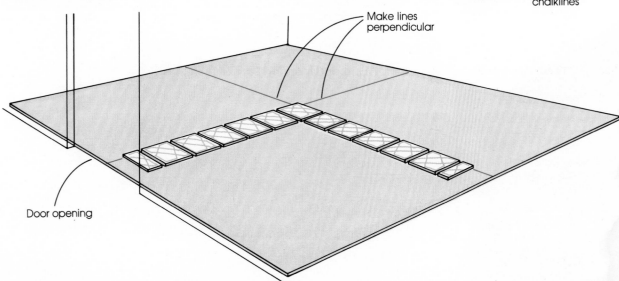

RESILIENT TILE FLOORS

Begin the first quadrant. Sweep and vacuum all dirt from the floor. Read the label's instructions to see if the adhesive is applied with a roller, brush, or toothed trowel. All adhesives have a particular "open time," which is the period during which tiles can be laid before the adhesive becomes too dry to make a good bond. For some adhesives, you'll only have enough time to set six or seven tiles; for others, you'll have enough time to set most of a quadrant in one application.

Begin in the center of the room and spread a specified amount of adhesive into one quadrant, being careful not to cover up the chalklines. Avoid spreading it too thick, which will cause oozing of adhesive between tiles; or too thin, which will prevent a good bond. Carefully position the first tile so that it is perfectly aligned with both chalklines. Set the next few tiles along each axis and then fill the area between the axes as you work

your way to the walls. As much as possible, avoid sliding the tiles into position—set them into place instead. Work very carefully, since minor errors can cause major alignment problems later on.

Finish the first quadrant. Continue laying tiles along each axis and filling in the area between them. If you come to any obstructions, such as corners, pipes, or posts, cut tiles to fit around them. Make a template out of cardboard and trace its shape onto a tile. Use dividers to duplicate intricate shapes. Resilient tiles can be brittle when cold. They are easier to cut if you briefly warm them in an oven or over a furnace.

Finish the remaining quadrants. Finish each quadrant in the same manner, starting in the center of the room and fanning out along both axes. As you proceed you will find that you have to walk or kneel on newly laid tiles. Lay a 2-foot by 2-foot piece of plywood over them

Installing the First Quadrant

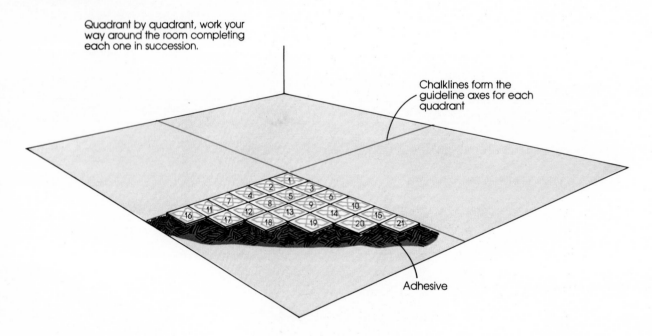

Quadrant by quadrant, work your way around the room completing each one in succession.

Chalklines form the guideline axes for each quadrant

Adhesive

Template Detail

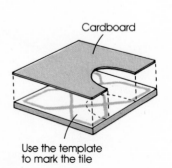

Cardboard

Use the template to mark the tile

Fitting and Marking Border Tiles

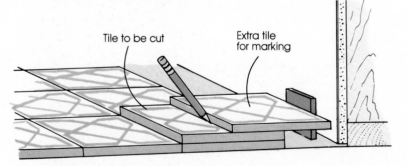

Tile to be cut

Extra tile for marking

to prevent displacing any tiles.

Be particularly careful about adhesive oozing out of the joints. Wipe it up immediately as you go, using a rag and compatible solvent. When you complete the floor, avoid walking on it until the adhesive has set. Check the manufacturer's instructions for setup time.

Cut border tiles. If you need to cut tiles to fit against a wall, mark each one in its place. First, set the tile to be cut directly on top of the last full tile in its row. Place a second tile on it and butt it up against the wall so that part of it overlaps the first tile. Mark the first tile by scribing along the second tile's edge with a pencil or blade. Cut the first tile with a knife, or score it and break it if it is too heavy to be cut. Then apply adhesive and install the tile. When the entire flooring field has been completed, install the finish details.

Vinyl cove base is an easy and attractive way to finish a resilient floor. Cove base is sold by pre-cut lengths. Each strip is fitted, cut to size if needed, and adhered to the wall individually. At inside corners you'll need to v-notch the flange and score the back of the strip so that it will bend to fit snugly to the walls. For outside corners, simply work the base around the corner; the flange will stretch enough to allow the material to wrap neatly around the projection. Apply adhesive to the grooved back only; don't adhere the flange to the floor itself.

Wood baseboards are a second option for finishing out the floor. If the baseboard material isn't thick enough to cover the tile-to-wall expansion gap, an added shoe molding will conceal it neatly.

Metal threshold strip finishes door openings or other areas where the tile meets an adjacent flooring surface. Simply nail it down to the subfloor taking care to avoid denting the strip as you hammer down the nails.

Installing Vinyl Cove Base

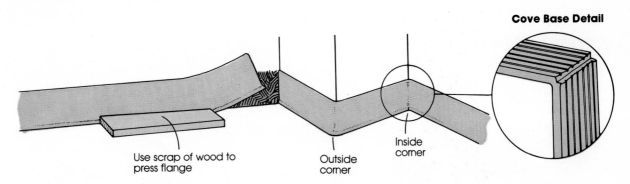

Use scrap of wood to press flange

Outside corner

Inside corner

Cove Base Detail

Installing a Wood Baseboard

Metal Threshold Strip

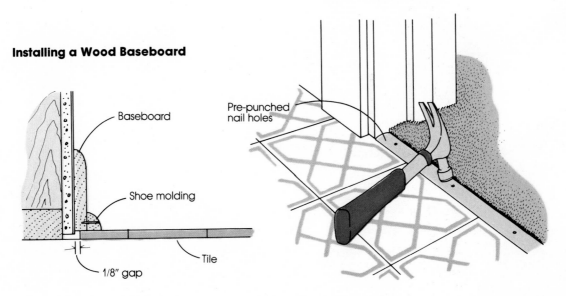

Baseboard

Shoe molding

1/8" gap

Tile

Pre-punched nail holes

CERAMIC TILE FLOORS

The procedures illustrated and described in these four pages are appropriate for uniformly colored tile floors and rooms with no special problems. For special situations—and for a general review of planning and layout—see page 61.

Snap chalklines. Tile installation usually begins along the most visually prominent wall and proceeds toward an exit so you can avoid walking on freshly laid tiles. Since the wall may not be straight, or may be out of square with the side walls, it is necessary to snap chalklines to work from. Begin by removing all baseboards and trim. Then measure out from the starting wall, at both ends, a distance equal to one tile width plus two grout lines. Make marks to indicate this distance and snap a chalkline between them.

Repeat this procedure for the other three walls, squaring each line to the previous chalkline by holding a framing square at each corner or using a 3-4-5 triangle (see page 60). When you have snapped all four lines, double-check for square by measuring both diagonals. You now have perimeter guidelines that will

ensure a straight row of tiles against the starter wall and will keep the starting end of each new row squared to the previous rows.

Try out the layout with a test run. Lay rows of loose tiles along each working line, from wall to wall. Set spacers between them for the grout spaces. Some tiles have lugs molded into their edges. If not, use special tile spacers available in a range of sizes, and sold at tile stores. The spacers should equal the thickness of the grout width you accounted for when you snapped the chalklines. This test run tells you whether tiles will need to be cut at the walls, and allows you to decide where you want to use cut tiles. You may be able to avoid cuts at one or all of the walls by simply altering the width of the grout spaces. If you alter the grout width in one direction, however, you'll need to do the same in the other direction as well. By experimenting with the test run you can find the layout that will be the most pleasing to look at and require the fewest cuts.

Nail down straightedges. To ensure perfect tile placement along the working lines, nail straight pieces of 1

Snapping Layout Chalklines

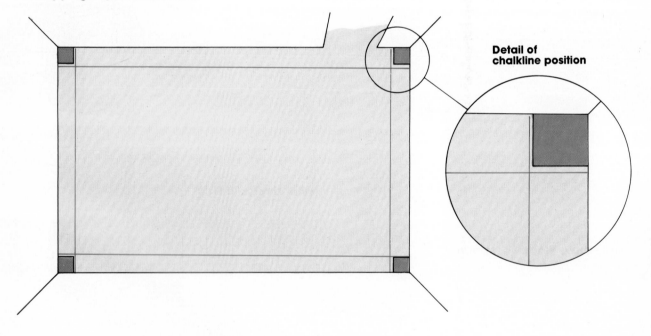

Detail of chalkline position

Nailing Down Straightedges

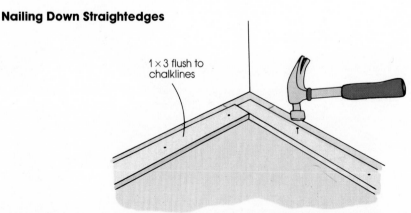

1 × 3 flush to chalklines

by 3 material, or straight strips of plywood, to the subfloor on the side of the lines closest to the wall. They needn't butt into each other at the corner, but their inside edges should align perfectly with the chalklines.

If you do not have grout spacers, you could also use these straightedges for layout sticks. Measure and mark the exact tile locations and grout widths along the length of each stick. As you set tiles further away from the stick, you can hold a framing square against the edge of the stick at each layout mark to align tiles out in the field.

Set the first row of tiles. Consult the adhesive package instructions to determine the troweling method and the recommended area for each application of adhesive, and use the type of spreading trowel recommended by the adhesive manufacturer. Spread no more than a square yard at first, until you get a sense of how quickly the adhesive sets up. Spread the adhesive right up to the straightedges and working lines, but do not cover them. If you are working with epoxy, be sure to wear gloves to protect your hands.

Set the first tile at the corner where the straightedges abut. Place the tile down onto the adhesive with a gentle twisting motion, but do not slide it into place. Butt it tightly against the straightedge. Complete the starter row, placing grout spacers between the tiles as you go. Molded plastic spacers can be left in place until you grout, but wooden or cardboard shims should be removed after the adhesive begins to set. Immediately clean off any adhesive that oozes onto the tile surface, using an appropriate solvent. Remove excess adhesive between tiles with a cotton swab or thin stick.

Finish setting the tiles. Start the second and all succeeding rows at the same end as the first. Butt each starting tile against the straightedge, and each succeeding tile in the new row against the installed row adjacent to it. Use molded spacers or shims wherever tiles meet, and check placements regularly with a framing square. "Beat" the tiles in as you go with a carpet-covered board and hammer to level the tiles with each other. Occasionally check the surface with a straightedge to make sure that it is even.

Applying Adhesive

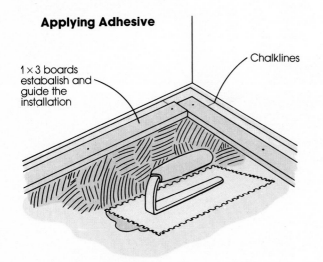

1 × 3 boards estabalish and guide the installation

Chalklines

Leveling the Tiles

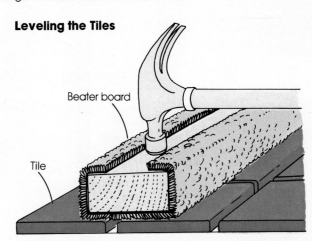

Beater board

Tile

Installing the Tile Field

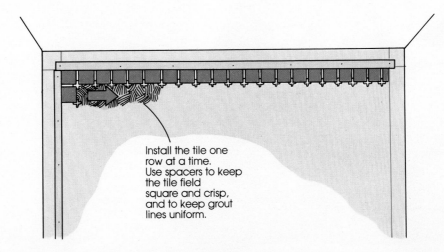

Install the tile one row at a time. Use spacers to keep the tile field square and crisp, and to keep grout lines uniform.

INSTALLING
CERAMIC TILE FLOORS
CONTINUED

You may have to cut tiles at the end of the row. If the layout is regular and perfectly square, and the tile spacing is consistent, cut several tiles ahead of time. Postpone any irregular cuts until the full row of tiles is set. Often, the dealer from whom you purchased the tiles will make the cuts for you.

If you have to kneel or walk on set tile, lay a small piece of plywood down to distribute your body weight more evenly across the surface. Finish the installation by removing the two straightedges and setting the remaining border tiles. Start at the original corner, and guide their placement from the existing installation, not the walls. Beat them into place and clean off any adhesive or dust.

Grout the joints. Remove any spacers and excess material from the cracks. Stay off the tiles as much as possible, since their edges are brittle and subject to chipping before being grouted. Mix the grout to a mayonnaise-like consistency, according to the manufacturer's instructions. Wear gloves to protect your hands. Dump a batch of it onto the tile surface and spread it into the joints with a rubber float, a tool you'll find at tile stores. Be sure the joints are tightly filled, with no voids or air pockets. If necessary, use an old toothbrush handle or similar object to pack the grout into the joints. Work the float diagonally across the field in both directions to scrape away excess grout. After 10 to 15 minutes, use a moist sponge to remove any remaining grout residue, rinsing and wringing it frequently as you go. When you have removed as much excess as possible with the sponge, let the grout dry for about 30 minutes.

After a film of dry grout appears on the surface of the tiles, wipe it off with a soft sponge or cheesecloth. This process also polishes the tiles. Use the toothbrush handle to tool and finish any joints that are not smooth. Allow the grout to cure according to the manufacturer's

Cutting Border Tiles

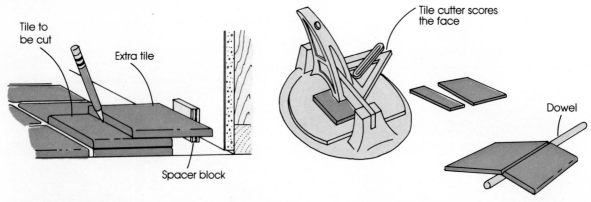

Tile to be cut · Extra tile · Spacer block · Tile cutter scores the face · Dowel

Grouting the Floor

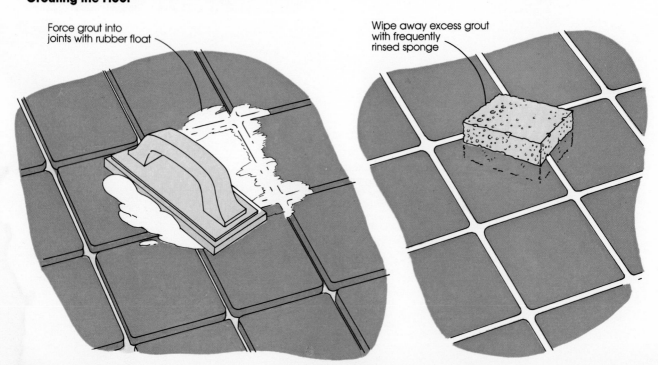

Force grout into joints with rubber float

Wipe away excess grout with frequently rinsed sponge

82

instructions. For best results, cover the freshly grouted installation with plastic sheeting for the first 24 hours. This way, it will not dry too fast which can cause it to crack.

Apply the sealer. Some types of tile and/or grout require a final coat of sealer two or three weeks after grouting. This is painted on, according to the manufacturer's directions. If you are sealing the tiles, use a large brush or paint roller to speed the process. If only the grout is being sealed, apply it to the joints carefully, with a small brush, and immediately wipe it off any tile surfaces with a damp cloth.

For a superb finish, give the floor a final buffing with a rented floor polisher.

Install baseboards or other trim. After the tile is installed, grouted, and sealed, you can nail wood trim around the wall edges. If the tiles are all level and the surface straight, the trim should snug tightly to the floor and leave no unsightly gaps.

If you are using floor tiles, such as large pavers, which have an irregular top surface, you can shape the bottom of the trim to follow the profile of the tiles. The easiest way to do this is to sharply bevel the bottom edge of the trim along the back, so that the bottom edge of the front surface is tapered to a thin wedge. Then set the trim piece in place and tap it down onto the floor. The bottom edge will crumple against the high spots of the tiles and conform to the exact profile of the tile floor. Check to see that the top edge of the trim is level, and nail it to the wall.

If you want a tile base around the floor, apply the tiles to the wall with adhesive at the time you install the floor. Use special cap tiles, or bull-nosed tiles. Place grout spacers or shims between the floor tiles and wall tiles, and between all the wall tiles. Grout and seal them using the same techniques used for the floor. See page 93, for more on installing tile borders.

Tailoring Grout Lines

Applying Sealer

Fitting a Wood Baseboard

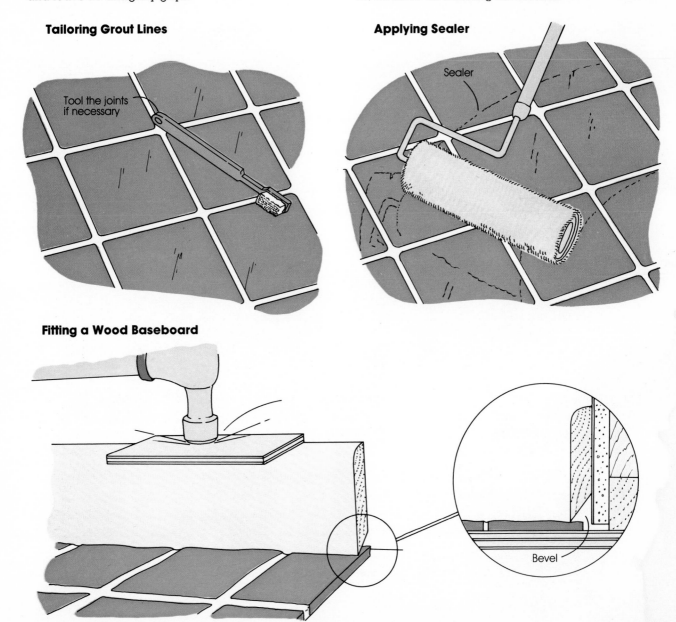

CONVENTIONAL CARPET

For most carpet installations, you don't have to remove baseboards, although you may later have to touch them up with paint or finish. Remove any doors that will be in the way of your work, after first marking trimming lines if the carpet will raise the floor level (see page 50).

Before you start, make sure that you have all the necessary tools and accessories needed for your installation.

Install the tackless strip. Use the type of strip specified for your carpet backing—type C for heavy backing, type D for Wilton and Axminster carpet, and type E for heavy latex or tufted carpet. If the strip will be anchored to a wood surface, use tackless strip manufactured with wood nails; if the surface is concrete, use tackless strip with masonry nails.

Starting in one corner, nail strip around the room's perimeter. Its pins should point toward the wall. Leave a gap between strip and wall equal to two-thirds the carpet's thickness. Cut pieces to length with a saw, shears, or strip cutter. Each piece should have at least

Installing Tackless Strip

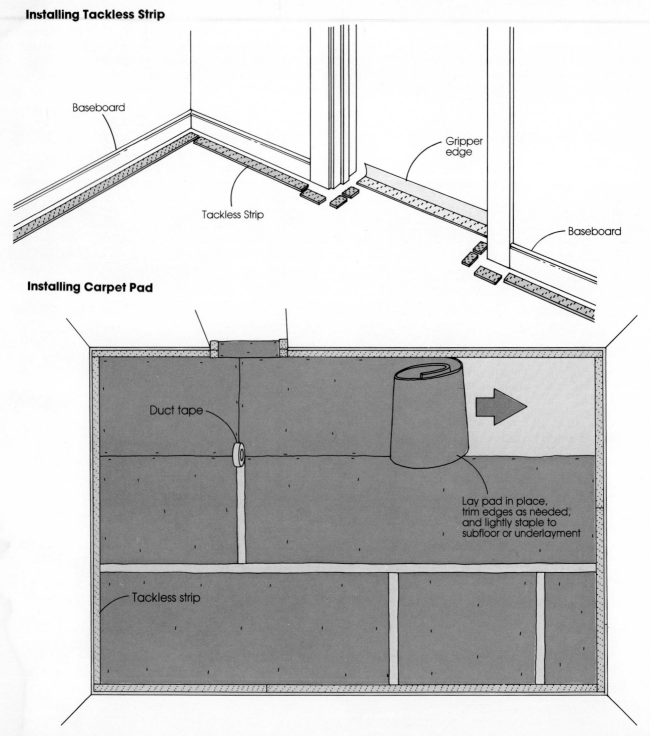

Baseboard

Tackless Strip

Gripper edge

Baseboard

Installing Carpet Pad

Duct tape

Lay pad in place, trim edges as needed, and lightly staple to subfloor or underlayment

Tackless strip

two nails holding it down; have extra nails on hand to fasten short lengths of strip. Follow all angles carefully, such as those around door casings or trim, and fit pieces around the perimeter of the room.

If you plan to nail tackless strip to concrete, test its holding power first. Drive a few nails into the slab around the edge. If they don't hold well, plan to glue the strip down with a special adhesive. Whether you are nailing or gluing strip to a concrete floor, there may be sections of strip you suspect may not hold. Add another row of strip in front of the first row in those areas.

If you are nailing into concrete with resilient flooring glued to it, the nails may not hold well, since the thickness of the flooring will reduce the nails' penetration and bite. If so, try tackless strip with longer nails, or scrape away a 2-inch margin of tile around the edge of the room and install a thicker tackless strip directly on the concrete.

To lay carpet over ceramic tile rough up the glazed surface with sandpaper to break the sheen and make a better bond. Then, glue down tackless strip in lengths equal to the tile unit.

Install the pad. Using a utility knife, cut a piece from the roll of pad, long enough to cover one end of the room. Position the piece just short of the tackless strip along its long edge. It should overlap the strip at both of its ends. Use a staple hammer to fasten it down every 6 to 12 inches around the edge of the entire piece. Staples should hold the pad firmly to the subfloor, but be sure that the staple tops do not puncture all the way through the pad. If the pad is waffled, staple into the depressions. Pull out any loose staples; they can work themselves up through the carpet later. To install a pad on concrete floors, fasten special paper tape around the edge of the pad so that it laps onto the pins of the tackless strip.

Continue cutting and fastening the pad until the entire floor is covered. Butt the edges; don't overlap them. To trim the excess at the edges, run a utility knife along the edge of the tackless strip; hold the knife at a slight angle to bevel the edge toward the strip. Increase the angle for a foam pad. This makes sufficient space at the edge so that the pad won't ride up onto the tackless strip during installation of the carpet.

Three Ways to Finish a Door Opening

Over Concrete Slabs

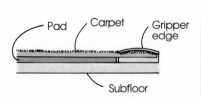

Over Nailable Surfaces

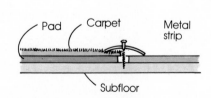

Invisible Binding

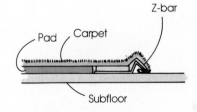

If the subfloor is concrete, nail a special gripper edge across the doorway using concrete nails to fasten it down. The teeth bite the carpet, and the curved metal flange is hammered down over the edge to bind the carpet's edge.

If the subfloor is a nailable surface, this type of metal strip makes a clean binding where the carpet you're installing butts an adjacent floor surface. Nail down the strip as shown in the illustration above. This type of binding, and the one shown at left, are both visible.

If you do not want a visible strip to bind the edge, and if your installation will accommodate this type of binding, consider using a special Z-bar. Nail it under a length of tackless strip installed in the door opening. The carpet wraps over the "Z" and is clinched by it.

Cut the carpet. Unroll enough carpet for the first piece that you will be cutting in an area where it can lay out flat. Be sure the cutting surface is clean and dry. If you need to protect the carpet from soil or moisture, lay down a sheet of plastic first. When you make the rough cuts, leave wall and seam allowances of 2 or 3 inches; these will be trimmed to fit later.

Before measuring the first cut, square the carpet end by folding it back 3 or 4 feet so that the side edges line up over each other. Measure the distance from the front corner back to the fold at both sides. These distances will be equal if the end is cut square to the side edges. If the measurements are not equal, square the carpet by measuring along the longer edge, starting at the fold, a distance equal to the shorter edge. Make a mark, and then make all measurements along that edge from the *mark* rather than the *corner*. Notch the mark so you can see it from the carpet's face.

If the carpet has loop pile in straight rows, cut it from the face side, using a row cutter or utility knife. Before making the cut, use a screwdriver to clear the cutting path by separating the pile rows.

Many carpets can be cut from the back. First, measure on its face along both edges and mark the points from which you will cut with a small notch or slit. Roll back the carpet far enough to snap a chalkline across its back between the two notches. Using a straightedge, cut with a utility knife just deeply enough to sever the backing. Separate the pieces carefully, cutting any pile yarn that holds the two pieces together.

Set the pieces in place. Unroll each piece so that its pile leans in the proper direction, with the first edge lapping slightly up the wall. At corners and obstructions make relief cuts by slitting vertically through the 2- to 3-inch waste portion of the carpet, just to the depth that allows the carpet to lie flat. Overlap pieces that will be seamed by an inch or so. Check to see that the pile of each piece is leaning in the correct direction.

Setting the Pieces in Place

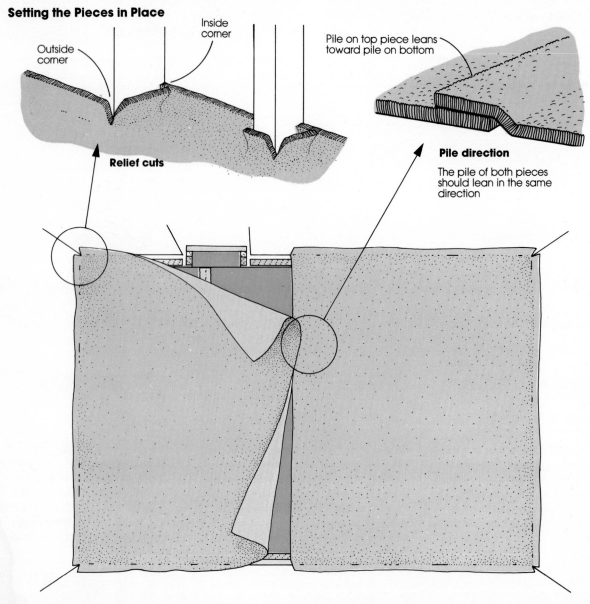

Outside corner

Inside corner

Relief cuts

Pile on top piece leans toward pile on bottom

Pile direction

The pile of both pieces should lean in the same direction

Cut the seam edges. On both pieces, cut the seam edges to be sure they are perfectly straight and parallel. For a loop pile carpet, position the pieces so that the edges are parallel, the pile of both pieces leans in the same direction, and the edges overlap at least 1 inch. The pile of the overlapping piece should lean toward the bottom piece. Using the edge of the overlapping piece as a guide, cut the bottom piece with a row cutter. Finish the cut with a utility knife at the edges where the carpet laps up the wall. *Note:* If the seam is in a doorway or other location where exact placement is necessary, stretch the first piece of carpet into place before trimming and making the seam (see page 88).

Seam the pieces together. Cut a length of hot-melt seaming tape to the exact length of the seam. Center it under the seam with the adhesive side up, by lifting one of the carpet edges and sliding the tape into place. Heat the tape with a special seaming iron or an old clothes iron warmed to 250°. Slip the iron onto the tape at one end of the seam and let both pieces of carpet flop onto the top of the iron. Glide the iron slowly along the tape, about a foot every 30 seconds, pressing the carpet edges tightly together along each just-heated section. Move the iron with one hand while holding the edges together with the other. Keep pile out of the adhesive and check to see that the backings butt tightly together. As you move away from each heated section, place some books or flat heavy objects on it to hold the seam together.

Continue seaming until you get as close as you can to the far wall. Let the seamed carpet set and cool for 5 or 10 minutes before rolling the edge back to expose the tape. Heat it and finish the seam. You may be able to avoid this delay by running the iron up the wall on the first pass, but if the seam edges do not abut perfectly at that time, the seam will be weak. Go back over the seam and groom it by cutting off any stray backing threads or loose pile ends with a small scissors.

Squaring the Seam Edges

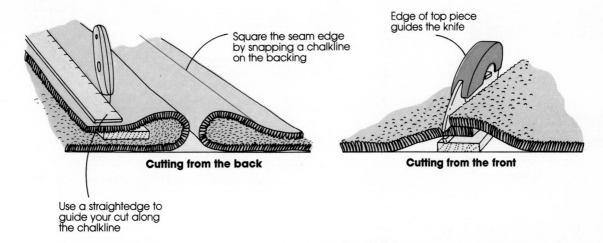

Square the seam edge by snapping a chalkline on the backing

Edge of top piece guides the knife

Cutting from the back

Cutting from the front

Use a straightedge to guide your cut along the chalkline

Positioning the Seaming Tape

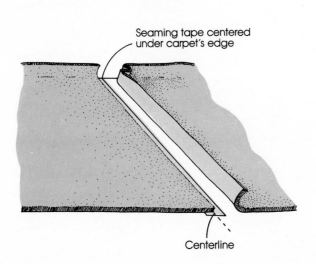

Seaming tape centered under carpet's edge

Centerline

Joining the Seam

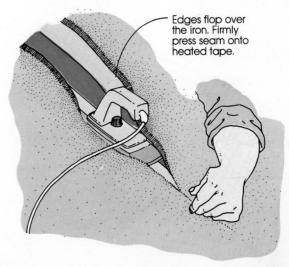

Edges flop over the iron. Firmly press seam onto heated tape.

Kick the first edge into place. Choose the wall you will be stretching the carpet away from and secure the carpet to the tackless strip by using a knee kicker. Before you start, adjust the kicker's tooth bite on a piece of scrap carpet so the teeth just penetrate the backing when you kick against the cushion with your knee.

To secure the first edge onto the tackless strip, bite the kicker's head into the carpet about an inch from the wall. Lean on the arm handle and swiftly kick its cushion with your knee. As you proceed, kick by kick, hold the secured carpet down onto the strip with your hand so it won't unhook. You may need to force it a bit with a stair tool or stretching paddle if the carpet is very stiff and won't fold tightly against the wall.

Stretch the carpet. See the diagrams for kicking and stretching patterns. For short distances, such as across hallways or small bedrooms, you can use the knee kicker to stretch the carpet into place. Use a power stretcher for full-size rooms. It has extension tubes that make it possible to stretch carpet across a room of any dimension.

Adjust the stretcher's teeth to your carpet's thickness. Set the head of the stretcher 6 inches from the wall and adjust its extension tubes so the foot presses against the opposite wall. Then press down on the lever to stretch the carpet toward the wall at the stretcher's head. The lever should lock down into place with a gentle and easy push. If the carpet does not move easily, lift the head and lower the handle a bit before biting into the carpet again. With the handle locked and the carpet stretched, fasten the section of carpet held by the stretcher's head down onto the tackless strip. Use the

How to Stretch the Carpet

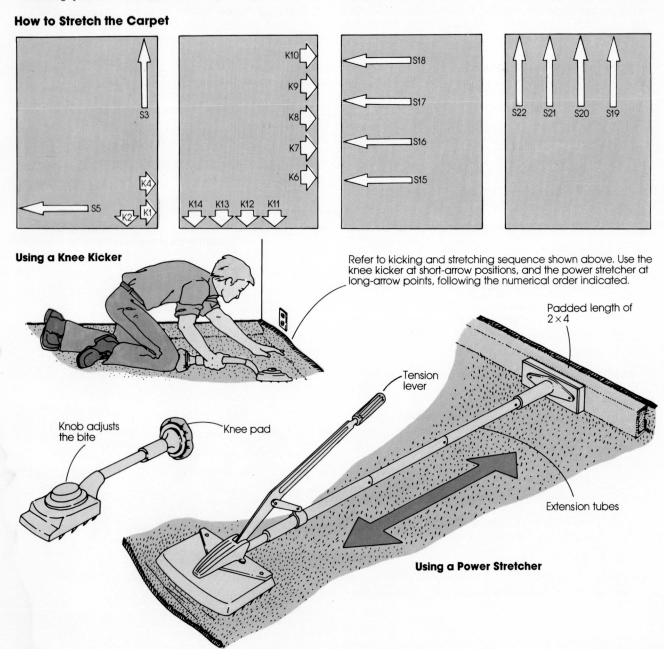

Using a Knee Kicker

Knob adjusts the bite

Knee pad

Refer to kicking and stretching sequence shown above. Use the knee kicker at short-arrow positions, and the power stretcher at long-arrow points, following the numerical order indicated.

Tension lever

Padded length of 2 × 4

Extension tubes

Using a Power Stretcher

trowel-like paddle that comes with the stretcher or the side of a hammer to push the carpet down onto the pins. Then release the stretcher's head, move it over 18 inches, and repeat the operation.

You or a partner will have to move the foot of the stretcher along the opposite wall as you proceed. Protect the baseboard or a weak wall with a piece of 2 by 4 long enough to span three or four studs. For added protection, cover the 2 by 4 with a piece of scrap carpet. Set it between the stretcher's foot and the wall.

Trim and tuck the edges. Trim the excess carpet around the edges with a wall trimmer adjusted to your carpet's thickness. Start at the lapped end of the carpet, slicing downward at an angle until the trimmer is flat against the floor. Then hold the trimmer against both the wall and floor, and plow along the carpet's edge. Care-

fully trim the last few inches with a utility knife. Tuck the trimmed carpet edge down into the gap between the tackless strip and the baseboard. Use a broad screwdriver or stair tool, pushing it into the narrow section of carpet lapping over the gap rather than down onto the very edge of the carpet itself. Otherwise, the carpet will bulge and lift off the strip pins. For stiff carpet, you may need to hit the screwdriver or stair tool with a rubber mallet to tuck the carpet into the gap.

At doorways, trim the carpet edge so that it centers under the closed door. If you installed a gripper edge on a concrete floor, flatten the metal flange over the carpet with a rubber mallet or a wood block and hammer. If you are covering the edge with a flat bar on wood floors, nail the loose edge of the carpet down first with tacks or 1-inch lath nails.

Trimming the Carpet to Fit

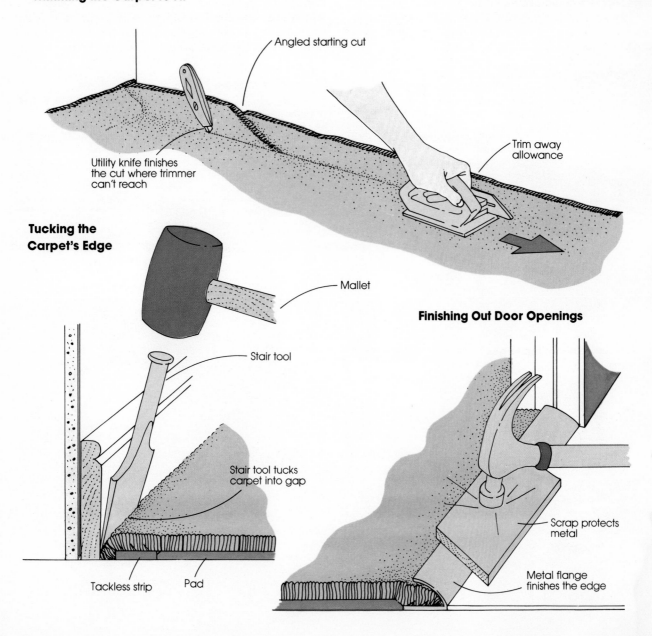

Angled starting cut

Utility knife finishes the cut where trimmer can't reach

Trim away allowance

Tucking the Carpet's Edge

Mallet

Stair tool

Stair tool tucks carpet into gap

Tackless strip   Pad

Finishing Out Door Openings

Scrap protects metal

Metal flange finishes the edge

INSTALLING
CUSHION-BACKED CARPET

Cushion-backed carpet has its own bonded foam backing. It requires no stretching since it is simply fixed to the existing floor with the appropriate adhesive. The existing floor needs to be prepared carefully, if the material is relatively thin, since irregularities in the floor surface immediately beneath it might be visible.

If the subfloor has open knotholes or gouges, they should be filled and sanded smooth. Board subfloors or tongue-and-groove floors will show through the carpet. Plan to install a minimum ¼-inch underlayment, and fill all the cracks and nailholes with floor filler.

Concrete subfloors must be completely free of moisture, since the carpet's foam backing acts like a sponge. If the problem is minimal, apply a coat of sealer to the subfloor. If moisture persists, do not lay the carpeting. The use of cushion-backed carpet over plywood floors on sleepers or nailed directly to concrete is not recommended; use conventional carpet instead.

You can lay cushion-backed carpet directly on a tile floor, as long as it is flat and dry and you fill all grout lines with a latex-type underlayment.

Install a toothless binder bar with a flange that clamps down over the carpet to finish the edge at door openings. If you need to seam the carpet, begin with the instructions for how to cut and place carpet pieces. If not, begin directly with the explanation of how to glue down the carpet, after you've rough-cut it to size.

Cut and place carpet pieces. Roll out and rough-cut the carpet, allowing a 3-inch margin at all floor perimeter edges. Cushion-backed carpet is always cut from the face. Snap a chalkline on the floor where the seam will be placed. Align one edge carefully to the chalkline, and place the second piece so that its edge overlaps the bottom piece by ¼ inch. Fold both the edges back about 2 or 3 feet, and trowel a thin, even coat of adhesive onto the exposed floor. Unroll the bottom piece into place, carefully keeping its edge aligned to the chalkline. Work the carpet with your hands to force air bubbles out to the edge.

Apply seaming fluid. Avoiding getting any on the pile, lay a bead of seaming fluid on the adhered piece of carpet along the edge of the primary backing material.

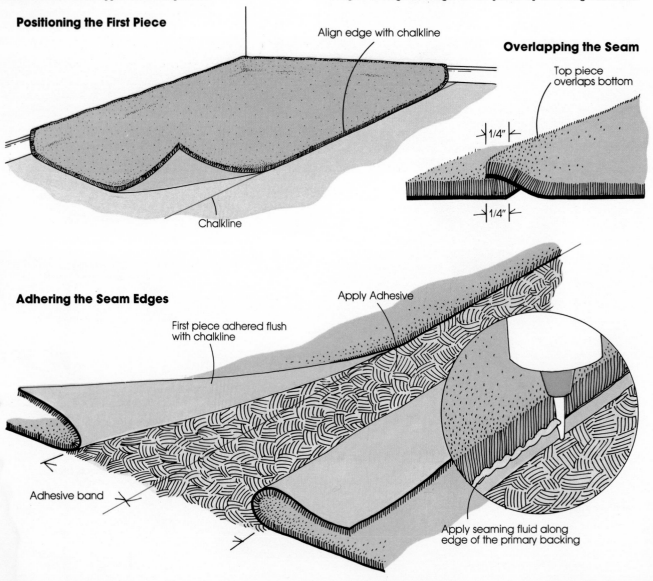

Positioning the First Piece

Align edge with chalkline

Chalkline

Overlapping the Seam

Top piece overlaps bottom

1/4"

1/4"

Adhering the Seam Edges

First piece adhered flush with chalkline

Apply Adhesive

Adhesive band

Apply seaming fluid along edge of the primary backing

Notch the nozzle so that when you run its tip along the floor, the bead is expelled at just the height of the primary backing, and not on the pile or foam.

Glue the seam together. Unfold the second piece of carpeting back so that its edge tightly abuts the adhered piece. Be sure any patterns line up. Since you allowed a quarter-inch overlap, the edges should press tightly against each other. The bulge produced by the allowance should be worked gently away from the seam. Where there are gaps, carefully rejoin both edges with your fingers until the entire seam is tight. Let the seam adhesive dry thoroughly before completing the installation. Snip off any loose ends of pile or backing threads.

Glue down the carpet. Starting from the side walls, fold each edge in so that the untrimmed carpet edges don't bind against the wall. Then pull the whole piece back to the already adhered seam area. If there is no seam, pull the single piece back until at least half the floor is exposed. Trowel adhesive onto the floor and roll the carpet onto it toward the wall, working out any wrinkles or bumps with your hands as you go. Repeat the process for the other half of the carpet. If you have to deflate a bubble, poke it with an awl. Then use a plastic syringe (which you can buy when you purchase the carpet) to inject contact adhesive into the hole, and press the carpet firmly onto the adhesive.

Trim and finish the edges. Trim the excess carpet by using a stair tool to seat and crease its edge well into the floor-to-wall joint. Use a utility knife to trim the carpet, leaving a margin equal to the thickness of the carpet around each wall's edge. Tuck that margin down against the wall with a stair tool. Flatten down any metal doorway flanges over the exposed carpet edge by placing a block of wood at one end and hitting it with a hammer, working your way across the flange. The wood will protect the flange from dents as the hammer bends it down tightly onto the carpet's edge. *Caution:* Some carpet adhesives are noxious or even flammable. Read the manufacturer's instructions carefully, and make sure the room is well ventilated. Extinguish nearby pilot lights and other open flames.

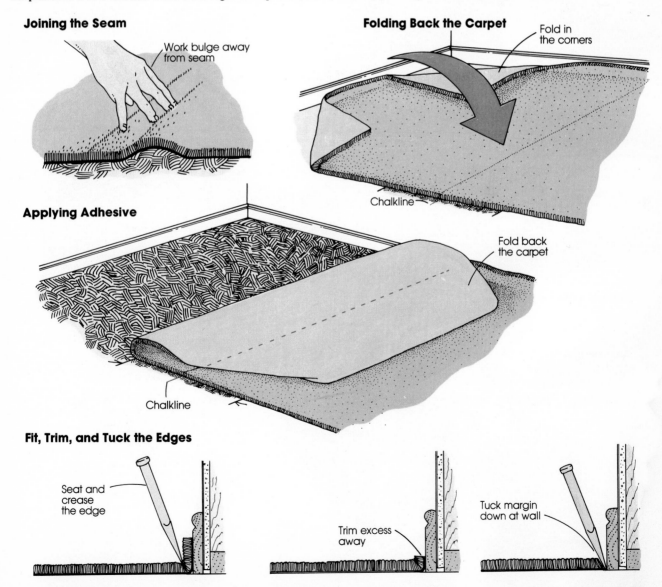

Joining the Seam

Work bulge away from seam

Folding Back the Carpet

Fold in the corners

Chalkline

Applying Adhesive

Fold back the carpet

Chalkline

Fit, Trim, and Tuck the Edges

Seat and crease the edge

Trim excess away

Tuck margin down at wall

INSTALLING
TRIM DETAILS

Baseboards, thresholds, and other trim and finish details are important parts of your new floor. Visually, they integrate the floor with the walls, and functionally, they conceal and protect the perimeter gap. When making selections you have many options, and they are generally a matter of personal preference.

Baseboard materials range from simple square-edge lumber to intricate wood moldings, vinyl cove base, and fancy ceramic border tiles. Wood and vinyl baseboard materials are bought by the linear foot, and each length is cut to fit as you go. Ceramic tiles are bought by the tile and installed individually. There are a variety of trim pieces to cover carpet or resilient flooring edges where they abut adjacent floors.

Thresholds are available in hardwood (usually oak), metal, and real or synthetic marble. Wood and metal are easy to cut to length. Both are fastened to the subfloor with screws or nails. Marble thresholds can be cut to size by the supplier, and are glued down with special adhesives.

Install wood baseboards. To install wood baseboards, measure each length of board carefully so that you can cut them to fit tightly. Wherever the boards join along the wall, cut the ends at 45-degree angles rather than square. That will prevent the joints from opening up as the material shrinks or the building moves. Make miter joints at all outside corners. Inside corners should have butt joints for square-edge boards and special coped joints for molded boards. Nail the boards in place at each stud, using 6- or 8-penny finish nails.

Install vinyl cove base. To install a new cove base, glue it to the wall, length by length, fitting and bending each

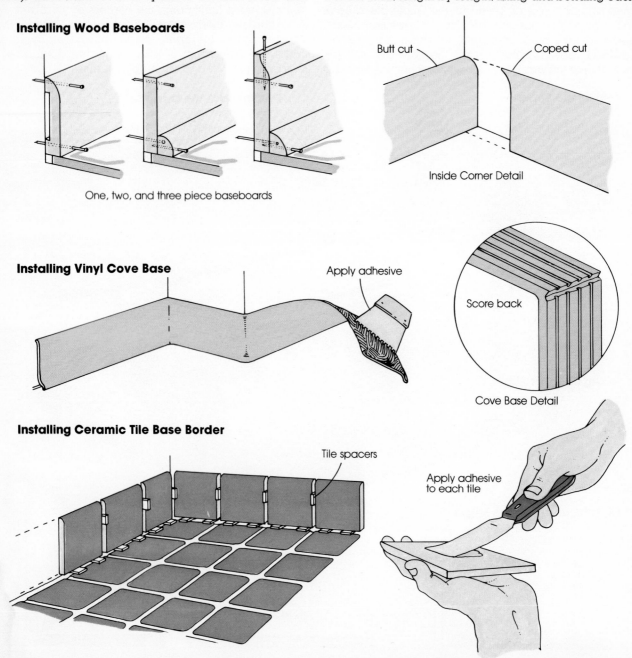

Installing Wood Baseboards

One, two, and three piece baseboards

Butt cut   Coped cut

Inside Corner Detail

Installing Vinyl Cove Base

Apply adhesive

Score back

Cove Base Detail

Installing Ceramic Tile Base Border

Tile spacers

Apply adhesive to each tile

piece as you go. To fit an inside corner, cut a V-notch in the base flange, and lightly score the back from the notch to the top edge.

To fit an outside corner, cut a V-groove down the back, removing excess material from the groove. Don't notch the base flange, since it will stretch to wrap around the corner. To install the cove base, use a notched trowel or putty knife to apply adhesive to the wall only as high as the base will cover. Or, apply adhesive directly to the back of the cove base. Press the base firmly into place.

Install ceramic-tile base borders. To install tile base borders, use ceramic tile with one bull-nosed edge so the border's top edge will be finished. After the floor has been installed, cut and fit each base border tile so that the floor's grout lines continue into the border.

Start in one corner. Dry-fit the first tile, and cut it to size to match the floor's grout line. Then apply adhesive to the back of the tile. Place spacers at the floor, and press the tile into place. As you mount each successive tile, use both side-spacers and floor-spacers to keep the grout lines consistent. Grout as shown on page 83.

Install thresholds. Before installing a new wood threshold, undercut door stops if necessary. Then cut the threshold to length, predrill pilot holes, and nail it to the floor with 8-penny finish nails.

Install reducer strips. When floors of different heights meet, you can use a wood reducer strip instead of a surface-fastened threshold. The reducer is bevel-cut so that its high edge is flush with the higher floor and its low edge is flush with the lower floor. This adjusts the new flooring level to the existing adjacent floor.

Undercutting Door Casings

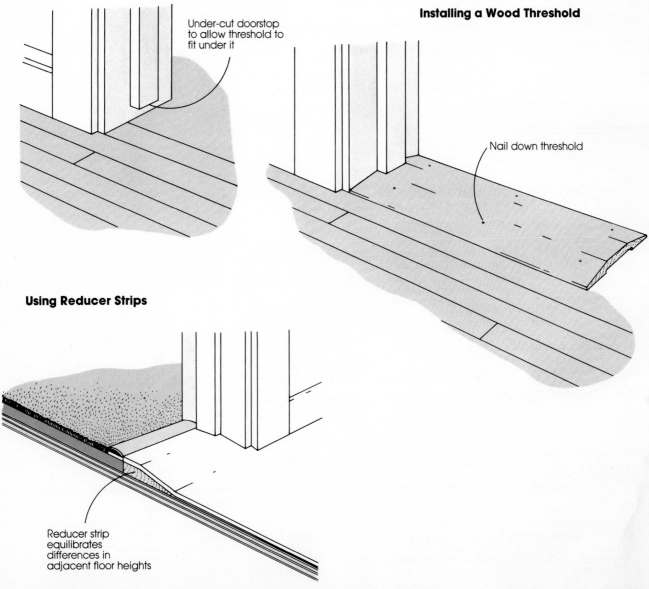

Under-cut doorstop to allow threshold to fit under it

Installing a Wood Threshold

Nail down threshold

Using Reducer Strips

Reducer strip equilibrates differences in adjacent floor heights

INDEX

Particle board, for
  underlayments, 57
Patterns, 8
  carpet, 28
  ceramic and masonry,
    24–25
  resilient, 19, 20, 21
Perimeter layout, 61
Pile direction, carpet, 31, 86
Planning, 34–37
  for carpet floors, 30–31
  for ceramic and masonry
    floors, 24–25
  for resilient floors, 18–19
  for wood floors, 12–13
Plugs, in wood floor
  installation, 67
Plywood, for underlayments,
  57
Polyester carpets, 33
Polypropylene olefin carpets,
  33
Polyurethane wood resilient
  floors, 21
Prefinished wood flooring,
  14–15, 65
Preparation
  for installation, 39–57, 62, 74,
    90
  for sanding wood floors, 70
Professionals, flooring, 34, 35

Q

Quadrant layout, 61, 68–69,
  77–79
Quarry tile and pavers, 26,
  27

R

Racking floors, 63
Radiant heating, 22, 48
Reducer strip installation, 93
Refinishing wood floors,
  70–73
Removing base borders and
  molding, 51, 52, 74
Removing doors, 50, 84
Removing existing flooring,
  52–53
Removing grease, oil, paint,
  dirt, from concrete slabs, 54
Removing stains, in wood
  floors, 72
Removing thresholds, 51
Resilient floors, 6, 16–21
  estimating materials for, 37
  installation of, 59, 74–79
  preparation for installing,
    40, 44–45
  removal of, 52
  selecting materials for,
    20–21
Reversing direction, in wood
  floor installation, 64
Rewaxing wood floors, 70
Rubber, for resilient flooring,
  21

S

Sanders, 71–72
Sanding wood floors, 70,
  71–72
Scale, 8
  of ceramic and masonry

floors, 24
  of resilient flooring, 19
Scratches, in wood, 10
Sealing ceramic floor finish, 83
Sealing resilient sheet seams,
  76
Sealing wood floor finish,
  72–73
Seaming fluid, with cushion-
  backed carpet installation,
  90–91
Seam placement
  in carpet floors, 31, 86–87,
    90
  with resilient sheets, 18, 76
Selection, of floor materials,
  5–37
Selection charts
  for carpet floors, 32–33
  for ceramic and masonry
    floors, 26–27
  for resilient floors, 20–21
  for wood floor finishes, 73
  for wood floors, 14–15
Sheen, of wood floors, 13, 59
Sheets, resilient, 18, 20, 21
  estimating materials in, 37
  installation of, 74–76
  preparation for installing, 44
  removal of, 52
Shoe molding
  installation of, 65, 75
  removal of, 74
Slate materials, 27
Snapping chalklines, 60, 61
  for carpet installation, 90
  for ceramic tile installation,
    80
  for resilient tile installation,
    77
  for wood floor installation,
    62, 68
Softwoods, 14, 15
Square-edge wood flooring,
  14, 42, 66
Squeaks, with wood subfloors,
  56
Stain application, in wood
  floor finishing/refinishing,
  72–73
Stain removal, in wood floor
  refinishing, 72
Starter-line layout, 61
Stone materials, 26–27, 41
Storing carpet, 48
Storing wood flooring, 42
Straightedges, with ceramic
  tile installation, 80–81, 82
Stretching carpet, during
  installation, 88–89
Structural changes, in
  subfloors, 41
Subfloors
  under carpets, 40, 48, 49, 85,
    90
  ceramic and masonry floors
    on, 22, 26, 39, 40, 41, 46
  preparation of, 39–57
  under resilient flooring, 44,
    45
  under wood floors, 40, 42,
    43, 62
Suppliers, flooring, 34

T

Tackless strip installation,
  84–85
Temperature
  masonry floors and, 22
  in resilient tile installation,
    78
  wood and, 42
Test runs
  for ceramic tile installation,
    80
  in resilient tile installation,
    77
  in wood block and parquet
    installation, 68
Texture, 8
  of carpet floors, 30
  of ceramic and masonry
    floors, 22, 25, 27
  of resilient floors, 19
Thresholds
  installation of, 65, 92, 93
  removal of, 51
Threshold strip installation, 79
Tile base, see Ceramic tile
  base borders
Tile units, resilient, 6, 16, 20,
  21
  designing with, 18–19
  estimating materials in, 37
  installation of, 77–79
  preparation for installing, 44
  removal of, 52
  See also Ceramic floors;
    Ceramic tile base borders;
    Parquet floors; Wood
    block floors
Time, installation, 59, 78
Tone, of floors, 6, 13
Tongue-and-groove wood
  flooring, 14, 15
  installation of, 62–65, 67
  nail schedule for, 42
  removal of, 52
Tools
  for carpet installation, 48,
    88–89
  for ceramic and masonry
    installation, 47
  for resilient floor installation,
    45
  for wood finishing/
    refinishing, 70–72, 73
  for wood floor installation,
    42
3-4-5 triangle, 60
Trimming carpet, 89, 91
Trimming doors, 50
Trimming resilient sheet
  flooring, 74–75
Trims, 92–93. See also
  Baseboards/base borders
Tucking carpet, during
  installation, 89
Tufted carpet, 32–33
Twist, carpet, 33

U

Undercutting, of door trim
  and casings, 51, 74
Underlayments, 40, 57
  for carpet floors, 90
  for ceramic and masonry

floors, 39
  removal of, 52
  for resilient floors, 16, 21, 44

V

Vinyl cove base
  installation of, 75, 79, 92–93
  removal of, 51
Vinyl resilient flooring, 6, 20,
  21

W X Y Z

Water, see Moisture
Weave, carpet, 32–33
Weight, of masonry floors, 22,
  26, 46
Wood baseboards
  installation of, 79, 83, 92
  planning and designing for,
    13
  removal of, 51
Wood block floors
  finishing/refinishing of,
    70–71
  installation of, 68–69
  planning and designing for,
    12, 37
Wood floors, 6, 10–13, 59
  estimating materials for, 37
  finishing/refinishing of,
    70–73
  installation of, 59, 62–69
  preparation for installing,
    40, 42–43
  removal of, 52
  selecting materials for,
    14–15
Wood-frame subfloors, 40, 41
  and carpet installation,
    49, 90
  ceramic and masonry floors
    on, 22, 26, 39, 41, 46
  over concrete slab, 55
  preparation of, 39, 41, 46,
    56–57
  resilient floors on, 44
  wood floors on, 43
Wood plank floors, 15
  finishing/refinishing of,
    70–71
  installation of, 67
  planning and designing for,
    12, 37
  removal of, 52
  subfloor preparation for, 40
Wood reducer strip
  installation, 93
Wood sleeper subfloors, 55
Wood strip floors, 14
  finishing/refinishing of,
    70–71
  installation of, 62–66
  planning and designing for,
    12, 37
  removal of, 52
  subfloor preparation for, 40
Wood subfloors, see Wood-
  frame subfloors
Wood threshold installation,
  93
Wood underlayments, 57
Wool carpets, 32
Woven carpets, 32, 33
"Wrapping," wood floor, 13

METRIC CHART

U.S. Measure and Metric Measure Conversion Chart

		Formulas for Exact Measure			Rounded Measures for Quick Reference			
	Symbol	When you know:	Multiply by:	To find:				
Mass (Weight)	oz	ounces	28.35	grams	1 oz			= 30 g
	lb	pounds	0.45	kilograms	4 oz			= 115 g
	g	grams	0.035	ounces	8 oz			= 225 g
	kg	kilograms	2.2	pounds	16 oz	=	1 lb	= 450 g
					32 oz	=	2 lb	= 900 g
					36 oz	=	2-1/4 lb	= 1000 g
								(1 kg)
Volume	tsp	teaspoons	5	milliliters	1/4 tsp	=	1/24 oz	= 1 ml
	tbsp	tablespoons	15	milliliters	1/2 tsp	=	1/12 oz	= 2 ml
	fl oz	fluid ounces	29.57	milliliters	1 tsp	=	1/6 oz	= 5 ml
	c	cups	0.24	liters	1 tbsp	=	1/2 oz	= 15 ml
	pt	pints	0.47	liters	1 c	=	8 oz	= 250 ml
	qt	quarts	0.95	liters	2 c (1 pt)	=	16 oz	= 500 ml
	gal	gallons	3.785	liters	4 c (1 qt)	=	32 oz	= 1 l
	ml	milliliters	0.034	fluid ounces	4 qt (1 gal)	=	128 oz	= 3-3/4 l
Length	in.	inches	2.54	centimeters	3/8 in.	=		1 cm
	ft	feet	30.48	centimeters	1 in.	=		2.5 cm
	yd	yards	0.9144	meters	2 in.	=		5 cm
	mi	miles	1.609	kilometers	12 in. (1 ft)	=		30 cm
	km	kilometers	0.621	miles	1 yd	=		90 cm
	m	meters	1.094	yards	100 ft	=		30 m
	cm	centimeters	0.39	inches	1 mi	=		1.6 km
Temperature	F°	Fahrenheit	5/9	Celsius	32°F	=		0°C
		(after subtracting 32)			68°F	=		20°C
	C°	Celsius	9/5 +32	Fahrenheit	212°F	=		100°C
Area	$in.^2$	square inches	6.452	square centimeters	$1\ in.^2$	=		$6.5\ cm^2$
	ft^2	square feet	929	square centimeters	$1\ ft^2$	=		$930\ cm^2$
	yd^2	square yards	8361	square centimeters	$1\ yd^2$	=		$8360\ cm^2$
	a	acres	.4047	hectares	1 a	=		$4050\ m^2$